MW00513794

IF YOU LOVE ME...

HOW YOU CAN KNOW FOR SURE THAT YOU LOVE GOD

DR. GEOFFREY C. PLUMMER

VEA PUBLISHING

JACKSONVILLE

© 2020 by

GEOFFREY C. PLUMMER

All rights reserved. No part of this book may be reproduced in any form without permission in writing from the publisher, except in the case of brief quotations embodied in critical articles or reviews.

All Scripture quotations, unless otherwise indicated, are taken from the *New American Standard Bible,* Copyright © The Lockman Foundation 1960, 1962, 1963, 1968, 1971, 1972, 1973, 1975, 1977, 1995. Used by permission. (www.lockman.org)

Scripture quotations marked ESV are taken from The Holy Bible, English Standard Version. Copyright © 2000, 2001 by Crossway Bibles, a division of Good News Publishers. Used by permission. All rights reserved.

Scripture quotations marked KJV are taken from the King James Version.

Cover photo source: jesusisreal.today, no creator noted.

We hope you enjoy this book from VEA Publishing. Our goal is to present the truth through thought-provoking books and products that connect truth to your real needs and challenges. For more information on other VEA Publishing books and study materials, go to veapublishing.com or write to:

VEA Publishing
P.O. Box 50235
Jacksonville Beach, Florida 32240

9 7 8 1 7 3 5 3 8 4 2 0 7

Printed in the *United Stated of America*

To my beloved bride Katherine with gratitude for her loving support, many prayers, and continual care.

To John MacArthur and the ministry of Grace to You for the dedication to sound doctrine and the countless supply of spiritual resources over many years.

To the unnamed many who have prayed for me and inspired me to continue learning and building teaching resources so that many would come to be makers of disciples

Contents

Introduction

The most recent Valentine's Day brought back a lot of memories of how I communicate my love for those in my family. How many times have I said the words "I love you" to my beloved spouse, our children, my extended family, and my brothers and sisters in Christ? When your heart has been changed by the gospel, your communication of love explodes, and so it had in my life over 30 years ago. While many men have issues in communicating their love for others, especially to other men, I was not so restricted. My relationship with my earthly father did not include any verbal expressions of love. It was not until I had moved out of the house that I ever heard "I love you" from him. That is not to say that I felt he did not love me, but, I must admit, I questioned his love for me many times. He was a difficult man to live with, and I was always struggling to live up to his expectations which seemed, to me, as requiring perfection. And I was far from perfect. As I grew up and began to make a life for myself, my father began to show that he cared by calling me from time to time, just to check in with me. It seemed a little unnatural at first, like, "Where have YOU been for the last 20 years?" Perhaps his advancing age had mellowed him a bit. With every child out of the house and my father's retirement a few years prior, he began to reach out more frequently.

1

My father contracted an oral cancer in 2010 and began his fight against a condition that resulted from a lifetime of poor habits. I travelled up to see him periodically and opened a dialogue with my siblings, finding that I was not alone. Their relationships with my father were just as confusing as mine was. I learned that I was called "The Chosen One" by my sisters since my father apparently showed me a much greater love than he did for them. I was the only boy, and my father always wanted a boy. When my father passed away in 2011 from congestive heart failure, his life had been changed because of his commitment to Jesus Christ as his Savior, and he and I were able to communicate many "I love you" moments in his final years. What I learned from those experiences was that my father had no real example of how to be a father, and my older sisters bore the brunt of that lack of example in my father's life.

After my father passed away, my Mum and I had many long conversations about how my father loved her. My Mum would watch me interact with MY children, and I would catch her smiling. "You are such an excellent father, Geoffrey!" she would say – which was soon followed by the statement, "You are nothing like your father!" My Mum experienced a similar relationship experience with my father as I did. It was a confusing relationship for her as well. "How did you know that he loved you?" I asked. "Well," she began, "...your father would do little things for me without me asking. So, I guess I just knew...but it wasn't easy." She and I frequently discussed my father's relationship with his own father, my grandfather. I found out that there was really no relationship there as my grandfather was a very difficult man. That insight reminded me of times in my childhood when I remember my father taking me over to my grandfather's house and escorting me inside, only to leave and go sit in the car while I visited with my grandfather. As I looked back, those events were very odd to me, even at age 6, but as the pieces came together in 2011, his actions began to make sense to me. I gave my father the benefit of a lot of doubts that year, and I fully believed that he did his best to show love for us. He just did not know how to do it. We all need that example of how to be loving parents and how to communicate that love to our children. So, I began to wonder how I had become a loving parent so different from my father, a quality my Mum recognized in me.

When I came to Christ, I fell in love with the story of "The Prodigal Son." I have preached on that passage many times, shared it with our children, used it as an example in counseling, and written about it in various Bible studies over the years. That passage in Luke 15:11-32 brings back many personal memories as I viewed myself as that younger son. As the years of being in Christ grew, I learned that every one of us is that Prodigal and that the story was not as much about the two sons but about the manifold love of the heavenly

Father. The vision Jesus created of the Father's love toward the returning son gave me the truest example of the loving father. Luke records, "But while he [the youngest son] was yet afar off, his father saw him, and was **moved with compassion**, and **ran**, and **fell on his neck**, and **kissed him**" (Luke 15:20)[1]. Those four highlighted actions gave me my definition of being a father. Keep in mind, the youngest son literally told his father he wished he was dead (Luke 15:12) since he wanted his inheritance NOW. You don't get an inheritance until your parents have died. Despite how the younger son treated his father, the father's love overwhelmed any prior statement, any circumstance, or any present condition in his life. The Father was moved with compassion, he ran, he fell on his son's neck, and he kissed him. If I had become a loving father as my Mum shared with me, this had to be the only way. Only through the example of the father of the Prodigal could I have come to understand what a loving father feels and what a loving father does.

When my children were younger, I would purposely take their hands in mine, wait until I had their complete attention, and then tell each one "You are a beautiful child, and I love you with all my heart." Even in the moments where they knew what was coming and even

---

[1] *New American Standard Bible* (La Habra, CA: The Lockman Foundation, 1977), All biblical references come from the NASB unless otherwise noted. All **highlights** in the book are author's additions.

when they began to mock me (my youngest daughter would see my eyes and mockingly say, "You're so pretty!"), I would continue communicating, sometimes adding in "You'll miss me when I'm gone!" I would have to correct her, "I did not say 'pretty,' I said "beautiful!" I could see the Prodigal's father feeling that same love for his child and making sure that he communicated that love through action. This parable was instrumental in my development and understanding of God, our example Father.

The Bible is replete with anecdotes and reasoning about how the Father loves us. I did not have any childhood memories of being taught to sing "Jesus Loves Me" like other children, although I did grow up attending church regularly. Instead, coming to Christ in my late 20s, I became an adult learner of Jesus's love for me. My beloved spouse sings "Jesus Loves Me" to our grandchildren when they begin to fuss or whine in the house. I'm amazed at how it calms them down immediately. There is something about the Father's love for us that is transformational. It should calm us, in every circumstance.

While the Bible is clear about how the Father loves us, how do we know we love Him? How does one really become sure they love someone else? Is it a guess? A gut feeling? An unusual emotional attachment? Ambrose Bierce was one of my favorite writers in college. He was a Civil War map man who went ahead of the Union army to map out territory in the South in preparation for battles. While he was away from his wife, she became lonely and started a relationship with another man. When Bierce returned home, he found that his wife wanted a divorce. Bierce became an extreme cynic and published a weekly column of definitions called *The Devil's Dictionary*. His entry on love was classical Bierce:

Love, n. Temporary insanity, curable by marriage.

While Bierce impacted me a great deal and added to my comedic personality, I do not want to reflect his cynicism about the nature of true love. Unfortunately, the question of how we really know we love someone remains shrouded in mystery to many today.

The goal of this book is to explain how we can know, for sure, that we love the Father, how we can know, for sure, that we love Jesus. I pray that you will come to know this truth and that you will be assured not only of His love for you but also of your love for Him. May He be glorified through the writing and reading of this book and may many be drawn closer to the Father who has compassion on us, longs to run to us, and loves to embrace us as His own.

DR. GEOFFREY C. PLUMMER

JACKSONVILLE BEACH, FLORIDA

Do You Love Me?

All the men attending that day knew it was Valentine's Day. What a good opportunity to have a message on love when we were in the tailwind of a Valentine's Day or on the brink of one. I began, "So, what I like to do on Valentine's Day is pick a random couple and have them come up on stage today and I will hand the microphone to the wife, and I will ask the wife to tell me how she knows her husband loves her." It was a simple request: "Tell me how you know your husband loves you!" As you can imagine, there were few volunteers that morning. Many of the men in attendance that day were staring at the carpet, no doubt pleading to God, "Please, Lord, don't let him pick me!"

What do you think about that question? What would your answer be if you are a spouse?

Would you be looking at the carpet, saying, "Please! Don't pick me! I want to just sit here and listen. Please don't pick me." I eventually let everyone off the hook, telling the congregation that no one would be put on the spot like that, but it did bring everyone's attention to the question of how we show love and how we know love. I did share a lot of information that I had gained from asking that question to various people in the past. I asked many wives in our church, "Hey, how do you know that your husband loves you?" It is a very interesting question because I got a lot of quizzical looks wondering why I asked the question. "Well, I'm just curious. I'm doing research," I would say. I'm like the Barna Group[2], just conducting my own Christian research study. I'm just asking the question, and I received very interesting answers to the question, usually three types of responses.

The first kind were historical answers, something like:

"Well, we've been together a long period of time and you know, and I, well, you know, he continues to work and serve and serve me and care for me and you know, and that's my definition of love."

Second, I got pragmatic answers, something like:

"Well, he hasn't left me yet. He's still with me. So, I guess he loves me."

---

[2] The Barna Group surveys and publishes reports on topics of Christian thoughts and church practices such as: "The State of the Church 2016 - Barna Group," accessed July 5, 2017, https://www.barna.com/research/state-church-2016/.

"He tells me he does!"

"He married me, right?"

Lastly, I got idealistic answers to that question akin to:

"Oh, I don't know. I just do!"

Those are interesting answers to that question. So, if I came to your house and asked you that question, what would you say about your spouse or partner?

How about if I asked, "How do you know that God loves you," how would you answer that question? Anyone who has a Bible, anyone who has had any Christian training, or anyone who had heard about the Bible at any level, or anyone who has experienced worship at a church should know categorically that God loves them, right? Amen? Pretty easy to see, eh?

How do you know if you love God is the other side of that question.

How would you respond?

Your answer may be historical: "Well, you know, I mean, I gave my life to Him at this point in time. I was baptized. I walked through this path of life, and I just know." Maybe your answer is pragmatic: "Well, I come to church every Sunday. I'm here. I get up and come to church." Maybe your answer is the idealistic: "Oh, I just do!"

Do you really love God?

Do you love God like God said you should love Him in the Old Testament?

> You shall love the LORD your God with all your heart and with all your soul and with all your might (Deuteronomy 6:5).

Is that how you love God?

Do you love God like Jesus said in the New Testament?

> 'YOU SHALL LOVE THE LORD YOUR GOD WITH ALL YOUR HEART, AND WITH ALL YOUR SOUL, AND WITH ALL YOUR MIND.' This is the great and foremost commandment. The second is like it, 'YOU SHALL LOVE YOUR NEIGHBOR AS

YOURSELF.' On these two commandments depend the whole Law and the Prophets (Matthew 22:37-40).

Is that how you love Jesus?

Maybe it would be better to have a realistic answer to that question from the Bible because the Scripture is very clear in saying how you can know, for sure, if you love God.

So, if I ask your spouse about the last Valentine's Day, "Did you tell your significant other that you love him or her?" – the answer is probably yes. Everybody reading this, I imagine, has told someone "I love you" in the past. You can probably even remember the first time you told somebody that you loved them. What was their reaction to you? Did they return your sentiment? What was your reaction when somebody told you that they loved you? Did you immediately return the favor and said, "I love you, too?" We tend to have reciprocal "I love you" statements, right? We naturally respond to many "I love you" statements immediately, as well.

Do we do that when God says He loves us?

Have you ever said, "If you love me…" to a spouse or significant other: "You know, if you love me, you will…" Or, if you have a child who needs to do homework, have you said, "If you love me, you'll get your homework done!" Or maybe you have mentioned to your spouse, "If you love me, you'll take out the trash." Or, "If you love me, you will rub my feet." Or, "If you love me, you'll just get out of my sight right now because I really can't deal with all of the stuff that's going on." In other words, "If you love me, you'll leave me alone."

When you hear "if you love me," what do you think of? Do you think that somebody is saying that they love you with a conditional love or maybe a manipulative love? Maybe you are trying to put a guilt trip on somebody and say, "You know, if you loved me you would do X, Y or Z."

Do you remember anyone in the Bible saying, "If you love me…"?

One Person immediately comes to mind: Jesus. Jesus said it simply, "If you love me, you will keep My commandments" (John 14:15).

Was Jesus trying to manipulate the disciples into compliance? Was He trying to ensure that they were true to Him before His departure and "guilt" them into staying the course? Was He trying to put them

in a corner and compel them to stand firm as He was leaving?

I do not believe Jesus was attempting any type of manipulation. The

definition of Jesus's love, shown through His exemplary life to these

disciples, did not need a subsequent and corresponding

manipulation, guilt trip, or forced adherence. He was not seeking to

diminish them ahead of His departure. He was, instead, giving them

a pathway to know for sure that they DID love Him. And we,

centuries later, can be assured of our love for God in the same way

these early disciples were assured: with five signs, five personal signs

that you can know, categorically, that you love the Lord, five signs

that, if they are true in your life, you should know and be assured

that you love the Lord. Every Christian should want to have this

assurance and be able to communicate it confidently to anyone in

their circle of influence as well. Let's walk together through these

signs and evaluate if our love of God matches what is expected of us

in the Bible.

Sign #1 – Obedience to His Commandments

The verses are recorded in Chapter 14 of John's gospel, a passage called the Upper Room Discourse. It is the most direct communication between Jesus and His disciples on record about God's eternal plan for Him, God's plan for them, and Jesus's immediate future. Jesus wants to make everything perfectly clear to His men before He leaves the planet. John records that Jesus hosted the first Lord's Supper with the Twelve where He exhibits true servanthood by washing their feet. Jesus then speaks of being betrayed and identifies His betrayer; Judas leaves the scene, and only Jesus and the eleven remain. Jesus tells them that He is about to be glorified and that He will only be with them a little while longer. The disciples soon realize that their version of God's plan will not come to fruition. "Wait a second, Jesus," you can almost hear Peter saying. "We left everything to follow You...and you're...leaving?" At that opportune moment when they are questioning their version of the plan, Jesus explains His plan for them by saying:

> A new commandment I give to you, that you love one another, even as I have loved you, that you also love one another. By this all men will know that you are My disciples, if you have love for one another.

The divine plan for them is to continue to set the example of the selfless love that Jesus displayed to them and would certainly be displaying to the entire world the next day. He says that it would be an identifying characteristic of their lives in that *all men* will know that they are His disciples. It is too much for Peter to consider. He has to get straight to the point: "Lord, where are You going?" Peter's boldness overtakes him: "Lord, why can't I follow you right now? I will lay down my life for You!" Peter is clearly not ready for Jesus to leave. The child in him is saying, "You've been with me for three years. I don't want you to go. I'm not ready for you to go." Jesus knows that Peter is ready but that Peter must face the ultimate challenge – his personal failure to live up to his boldly stated commitments. Soon, Peter will deny the Lord three times. Jesus's words put Peter back into his place and also refocuses the minds of other ten disciples since Peter was the oldest and their *de facto* leader. Jesus can then pour more encouragement into them.

At the beginning of Chapter 14, Jesus says:

> Do not let your heart be troubled; believe in God, believe
> also in Me. In My Father's house are many dwelling places;
> if it were not so, I would have told you; for I go to prepare
> a place for you. If I go and prepare a place for you, I will
> come again and receive you to Myself, that where I am,
> there you may be also.

Jesus tells them not to be troubled because there is a future place for them, saying, in effect, "I am going to come back for you. Don't worry about it now. You're ready to take over, and I have your back." Then Thomas asks a question of Him, "How do we know the way?" In other words, he asks, "How do we know where you're going? How do we know the way?" "Where" and "How" are good questions. Jesus had already answered the question in verse 3: "I AM the way." In other words, "You men get it. You eleven have a solid relationship with Me, and you stick with Me. I am the way, and when your time is at hand, I'll come back and get you." Philip is more direct with his request when he states, "Show us the Father." Show us the Father, and it's good for us, Philip says. Can you imagine the look on Jesus's face when Philip says, "Show me the Father." Can you hear Jesus saying, "You've been with me for three years, and you don't know that I am God?" Jesus is the same as the Father. Jesus and the Father are one. The disciples are plugged in to the Source, even if they do not recognize it. "If you ask Me for anything in My name," Jesus says, "I will do it."

Then Jesus utters the phrase of great significance (John 14:15):

"If you love Me, you will obey My commandments."

What, Jesus?

"If you love Me…"   <pause...>

"You will obey My Commandments!"   <boom!>

Afterward, Jesus spends a good bit of time discussing the coming Holy Spirit, the Presence that will be coming to the eleven to assist them in ministry.

It is quite easy to read through John 14:15 without thinking about what Jesus said. The interpreters and translators who put together the paragraph forms of the different versions of the Bible did not agree on the location of this verse. In the King James Version of the Bible, the verse is located with all the other verses of John 14 without separate paragraphs. It depicts a straight stream of consciousness recording the words of Jesus. In the English Standard Version of the Bible, John 14:15 is located with the verses that follow where Jesus discusses the Holy Spirit. In the New American Standard version of the Bible, the verse stands on its own, between two paragraphs. These differences highlight the fact that Bible translators might disagree about what Jesus means when He utters the phrase. Interpreters of John 14 are not sure about the verse's association with the content of the entire passage. Someone could study the Bible for a long period of time and still be unclear about the meaning and reasoning of a particular, seemingly critical, verse. Jesus stated,

"If you love me, you will obey My commandments" as part of one of the final teaching discourses for His disciples. These were to be lasting words in the mind of the initial disciples. The last time He was together with the Twelve, He made sure to include this statement which highlights its importance for them as well as for us.

Is Jesus being manipulative? Is He saying, "Look guys, there are eleven of you remaining. One guy we just kicked out. He's gone! Satan entered into him, and he's out. He is probably getting a payout of blood money at this very moment. So, I have you eleven now to work with...and you guys...**IF** you love me, this is what you will do." Is Jesus preying on the disciples with manipulation?

Is He trying to get them to obey with some sort of a guilt trip in mind? "Well, **IF** you don't obey Me, then I guess you must not love Me. I guess I need to go find some other guys that can cut it because if you can't obey Me, then I'll have to cut you loose!"

If you are one of the eleven who remained and had dedicated your life to this man's teaching for three years, how are you going to react if He says that to you...IF you love me? Are you going to interpret that statement negatively?

No, Jesus is not being manipulative. He is not attempting to coerce these eleven young men. This verse does not mean Jesus is putting a guilt trip on them to chide them into obedience. It also does not mean that there's some conditional aspect of Jesus's love here.

There is a reason why the Holy Spirit is mentioned by Jesus before and after John 14:15. What Jesus says in that verse is that **IF** you love me, certain characteristics will manifest themselves in your life. These characteristics **WILL** show up in your life. The Holy Spirit is the One Who makes those characteristics show up. That's why He is mentioned before and after this verse, at the beginning of that section of Scripture and at the end. It is not a guilt trip, nor does it have a manipulation emphasis. It is not some attempted coercion. It is a proof and a personal sign so that you **know** you love God if those characteristics show up in your life. Categorically, you can know if those characteristics manifest themselves in your life. Specifically, you will find yourself – almost without intentional thought – obeying Jesus's commandments.

Well, how does that obedience show up in a believer's life?

The moment you commit yourself to the Lord and grant Him access to your life, when you pray a prayer of salvation, when you ask for

His forgiveness for your sins, when you are willing to turn from your old way of living and look forward to a new way of living, the Holy Spirit comes to live inside. When the passionate movement of your heart at that point in life is to throw down a gauntlet and make a serious change, your journey begins. You have come to Jesus.

In John 14:16, the very next verse, Jesus says:

> I will ask the Father, and He will give you another Helper, that He may be with you forever; that is the Spirit of truth, whom the world cannot receive, because it does not see Him or know Him, but you know Him because He abides with you and will be in you.

In that first step in your journey, Jesus also comes to you. The Holy Spirit comes to live inside of you. Jesus says that He will give you another Helper that He may be with you forever. He will abide with you and will be in you. The very Spirit of the Living God comes to live inside us when we come to Jesus. You begin a new journey of sanctification as the Holy Spirit comes to indwell you, and He begins to transform your life, day by day.

If you are already a Christian, do you remember when you came to Christ? Do you remember the first time you went to the church? After church was over, you then walked out of the church, and you were back in the world. If the color red signified how much sin and the muck of the world was in you and the color white signified how much of the Bible and Jesus was in you, what would that combination of colors look like in your life in those early days? Maybe 95% would be red and only 5% would be white? The Holy Spirit's coming to live in us does not mean that we immediately give up every sinful thought and action right away. For me, that mix of colors was mostly red with a little speck of white. I was young and naïve, and very few of my thoughts were biblically minded.

But over time as you walk with Jesus in life and as you listen to Him through the study of His word, that white amount increases and increases, and the red in you fades away. If you are like me and my experience, I was praying hard that the red would get out of me immediately and the white would overtake me quickly, but that's not the way it happens. In 2 Corinthians 3:17-18, Paul wrote:

> Now the Lord is the Spirit, and where the Spirit of the Lord is, there is liberty. But we all, with unveiled face, beholding as in a mirror the glory of the Lord, *are being transformed* into the same image from glory to glory, just as from the Lord, the Spirit.

As we gaze at the glory of the Lord, we are being transformed from glory to glory through the influence of the Spirit...glory to glory. So, my brothers and sisters in Christ, you should see some level of growth in you where you see the light of Jesus taking over and the red evil of the world fading away. When that change happens in your life and when YOU begin to observe it in your life, you will KNOW that you love God. You WILL know it's not some fake commitment you made walking down an aisle or praying a prayer. Instead, you will know it is real and realize that the transformation of your life is under way and true sanctification has begun.

So, you may ask, "What happens if I believe I have committed my life to Christ, but I do not observe these events occurring in my life? Am I not truly saved?" Perhaps, the answer is yes. But, perhaps, the answer is no. Sanctification can occur without our knowing that it is happening, and other Christians may observe changes in you that you do not perceive yourself.

I often receive questions like, "I gave my life to Christ, but I do not feel any differently – did I do something wrong? Did I not do it right?"

An older lady named Sarah was determined to be saved. She committed her life to Christ five times in a single year, walking the aisle at her church to see her Pastor standing there each time with a quizzical look on his face. Why five times? She just wanted to be

SURE! But, after the fifth time, I approached and asked Sarah, "Do you not know that you are saved?" She began to weep. "I'm getting on in years, and I just want some assurance...that Jesus knows I'm sincere." I led this precious lady on a journey through her experiences in life by asking her if she felt differently now than she did in the past. I asked her if she perceived herself as more loving to others than in the past. Was she more caring and accepting of people? Was she more patient, more kind, more gentle to others, and more peaceful? She smiled and discussed how, in the past, she was very harsh and angry at people who wronged her. She held grudges. I asked her, "So, Sarah, when did that change in your life?" She mentioned that it happened over time and that she eventually realized that people are mostly the same and have the same needs and problems. "I guess I mellowed a bit as I aged," she said. "No," I told her, "you did not mellow with age. I know many people in life who age with anger and frustration, and they continue to lash out at people. It is not age that mellowed you."

I opened the Bible and led her to Galatians 5:22-23:

> But the fruit of the Spirit is love, joy, peace, patience, kindness, goodness, faithfulness, gentleness, self-control; against such things there is no law. Now those who belong to Christ Jesus have crucified the flesh with its passions and desires.

I told her, "Sarah, you did not mellow with age. You have the Spirit of the Living God in you, and He is transforming you, day by day, into the image of the Son because all of these characteristics are now apparent in your life. You see that in yourself, right?" She smiled broadly and thanked me for reassuring her of her salvation, and she promised not to walk the aisle again. Sometimes we need someone to remind us of what we should already know. If you find yourself changing positively from the way you have lived in the past, it is THE indicator that the Holy Spirit is at work in your life. If the fruit of the Spirit is showing up in your life, others may see it even if you do not. As Paul wrote in Ephesians 2:8-10, we are saved by grace which was nothing that we did ourselves, and "we are His workmanship, created in Christ Jesus for good works, which God prepared beforehand, that we should walk in them." We are to start walking in a new way, living differently, and seeking to be more loving, more joyous, and more at peace. This is why it is so important to walk with believers of every age and encourage them to show love and perform "good works" because the Spirit is made manifest in these events.

Paul wrote, "Therefore, if anyone is in Christ, he is a new creature; the old things passed away; behold, new things have come" (2 Corinthians 5:17). The old life is still there, but the new life is taking over. It is as if you are taking off one set of clothes and putting on a brand new set. That is how we know, with certainty, that we are His children, that salvation has truly happened, and that we have begun to love God. We begin to follow His commandments.

The Oxford English Dictionary defines faith broadly but provides insight to the kind of faith in Jesus I am discussing, noting:

> That kind of faith (distinctively called saving or justifying faith by which, in the teaching of the N.T., a sinner is justified in the sight of God. This is very variously defined by theologians, but there is in general agreement in regarding it *as a conviction practically operative on the character and will*, and thus opposed to the mere intellectual assent to religious truth (sometimes called speculative faith)[3]

True saving faith in Jesus <u>should</u> change your life. Justifying faith should not simply be an idea but should have a transformational effect on your character and will, that is, on your choices. You should see differences and feel differences.

However, if it does not happen in your life and you are not perceiving any changes in your life, then you should be concerned, right? If you are simply thinking and behaving the same way and there is no

---

[3] "Home: Oxford English Dictionary," accessed June 20, 2020, https://oed.com/. Emphasis added.

visible confirmation of a change in you to anyone else, then you need to consider your commitment to Jesus. This lack of change should be a sign to you that something may not be quite right in your life as a believer. If reading these last few lines gives you some level of concern, then now might be the opportune time in your life to pause and reflect on your life.

Do you truly want to commit your life to Jesus? Are you willing to ask Him for forgiveness of your sins? You probably know the facts of Jesus's life. He came to Earth, willingly filling the role that the Father asked Him to fill. He <u>lived</u> a perfect life. He <u>was</u> sinless! He gave His life on the cross, dying in our place, for my sins and for your sins. He was the sinless sacrifice so that He could become the door, the gateway to the Father, so that we could accept Him as Lord of our life and be rescued, saved from the eternal death that will come to anyone who does NOT accept Him as Lord.

Romans 6:23 says, "The wages of sin is death." If you live your life on the Earth without ever accepting Jesus as Lord, your payment will be death – eternal death and separation from God. But Romans 6:23 also says that "the gift of God is eternal life in Jesus Christ, our Lord." If you accept Jesus as the Lord of your life, you will receive eternal life, a gift of forever being in the presence of God.

If you are sincere in wanting to have that eternal presence with God, tell him so right now. Say,

> Lord Jesus, I admit that I am a sinner and need your forgiveness. I believe that Jesus died in my place, paying the penalty for my sins. I am willing, right now, to turn from my sin and accept You as my personal Savior and Lord. I commit myself to You and ask You to send the Holy Spirit into my life, to fill me and take control of my life, and to help me become the kind of person You want me to be. I want to see change in my life! Please make it happen! Thank you, God, for loving me, in Jesus's name. Amen.

With that one step, fully believed and sincerely spoken, you have begun your journey with Jesus and have assurance that God will do what you ask. The transformation of your life will have begun.

If you see the characteristics of your life changing, and if you can look into your past experiences and see how you've grown closer and closer to God, then you know He is at work in you. Paul wrote, "For I am confident of this very thing, that He who began a good work in you will perfect it until the day of Christ Jesus" (Philippians 1:6). The Holy Spirit does not begin a work in you and then stop the work. He will continue to work in you, if you are truly His child. No one willingly grows closer to God without the Holy Spirit's influence in his or her life. The prophet Isaiah wrote, "We all, like sheep, have gone astray, each of us has turned to our own way" (Isaiah 53:6). Paul wrote that "there is no one who understands; no one who seeks God" (Romans 3:11). A change in heart simply <u>does not happen</u> without the Spirit's influence.

So, if you've seen how the darkness of life has faded away and observed that the light is taking over, you have experienced a miracle. It should be miraculous to you when you realize these changes have occurred. You come into a new life with a fresh view and say, "Wow. I'm really obeying His commandments! When did THAT happen?"

So, Jesus's words in John 14:15 were not meant to be manipulative but assuring. The outward changes are reflective of what is happening on the inside. That is the main point when He says, "If you love Me, you will obey My commandments." Jesus was not finished teaching the disciples about the main point of the passage, however. As John continues his record in John 14:21, Jesus takes His teaching to the next level and says:

> He who has My commandments ***and obeys them*** <u>is the one who loves Me</u>; and he who loves Me will be loved by My Father, and I will love him and will disclose Myself to him.

The Apostle John expounds on Jesus's teaching in his first epistle, writing:

> By this we know that we love the children of God, when we love God and observe His commandments. <u>For this is the love of God</u>, that **we obey His commandments**; and His commandments **are not burdensome** (1 John 5:2-3).

These verses show that there is another level to the test of your love for God. He says that, by this test, "we know that we love the children of God when we love and observe his commandments." "Observe" can be translated as *obey*. It can also be translated as *keep*. Some people like the word "keep" a lot better than they like the word "obey." "Obey" seems to have a bad connotation as if it is very restrictive. But all the translations have the same meaning: we are to follow the directives that Jesus told us to follow. John is writing the same sentiment to his small flock in Western Turkey that Jesus, sixty years earlier, is mentioning to the remaining eleven disciples in Jerusalem. But John adds an important clause at the end of his message to his flock: our obedience to Jesus's commandments should not be burdensome. Following what Jesus says should not be burdensome to the believer! So, if you view your identification as a Christian as having a list of actions that you cannot do, and it pains you to keep from doing them, you fail John's test. If you explain the

Christian life to someone else and say, "You can't do this, and you can't do that. You can't do what you want to do. You can't do what unbelievers can do," the Apostle John would say that the love of God is not in you. You simply do not love God. As one of our congregation wrote to me, she learned "you can't dance, drink, cuss, or chew or hang around with those that do." If that is your attitude, then following Jesus is a burden. If you're thinking, "I can't do what I want to do because I have to stay in line or I'm out!" That is not how those who love God are supposed to view their lives in Christ. If that's you and your view of Christianity is "I can't do this. I can't do that. I am required to go to church every Sunday, every Wednesday night, and every other time the door is open. I have to participate in all these activities just to stay right with God," John is saying that is not the love of God in action. Believers should WANT to come together, support each other, care for each other, and be challenged by each other. Life is a journey that is to be shared with those on the same path as you. But if you feel that being part of the church is a burden, then something completely different is at work in your life, reflecting that guilt may be the driver to your obedience. John would tell you that your experience is certainly not reflective of a true love for God.

Coming willingly without a feeling of burden, however, is indicative of your love for God. If you love to come and if you love to spend time in fellowship with other believers, that is a positive sign. If you love to hear about Jesus's commandments, learn of His teaching, and love to see brothers and sisters in different phases of their spiritual growth, you should be assured. That should be your personal sign from the Lord that you are His and that you love Him.

Sign #2 – The Study of His Word

When I was much younger, I was given some good career advice: I should avoid three career paths because they were the most hated professions in the U.S.A. First, I was to avoid anything to do with money and taxes because people hated writing checks to others and paying taxes. Second, I was to avoid becoming a lawyer because people hated lawyers and created one-liner jokes like, "You know what a thousand lawyers at the bottom of the ocean is? A good start!" Lastly, I was to avoid becoming a doctor because people hated going to the doctor. If I avoided all three of those career paths, I would do just fine. Well, I must have been a rebellious youth. I look back on my educational transcripts and find that I have a degree in Financial Accounting, a Law degree with a specialization in Taxation, and a Doctorate degree. I have met each criterion to become one of the most hated men on the planet – just like Jesus did in His day! OK, perhaps not in the same way. Jesus probably did not have a background in accounting and taxes, nor did He obtain any doctoral degree, but we DO know that He loved the law.

Jesus said, "If you love Me, you will obey *my commandments*." Commandments to the Jews meant laws. It is difficult to say that you obey a law unless you actually know what the law says. Observing the law implies that you have voluntarily complied to a law that you are aware exists. Yes, it is possible that you keep from breaking a law by accident. No one had to teach me not to murder someone when I was seven. Most often, though, we learn what the laws are and then we commit not to break them and thus, we obey the law. The corollary point from Jesus's statement was that those who love Him will first <u>know</u> the law and then <u>obey</u> the law. In order to know the law, you have to study the law. To continue in the study of the law is to love it.

The Psalmist wrote:

> O how I love Your law!
> It is my meditation, all the day.
> Your commandments make me wiser than my enemies,
> For they are ever mine.
> I have more insight than all my teachers,
> For Your testimonies are my meditation.
> I understand more than the aged,
> Because I have observed Your precepts.
>
> I have restrained my feet from every evil way,
> That I may keep Your word.
> I have not turned aside from Your ordinances,
> For You, Yourself, have taught me.
> How sweet are Your words to my taste!
> Yes, sweeter than honey to my mouth!
> From Your precepts, I get understanding
> Therefore, I hate every false way.
>
> Your word is a lamp to my feet

And a light to my path.
I have sworn and I will confirm it,
That I will keep Your righteous ordinances.
I am exceedingly afflicted
Revive me, O LORD, according to Your word.
O accept the freewill offerings of my mouth, O LORD,
And teach me Your ordinances.

My life is continually in my hand,
Yet I do not forget Your law.
The wicked have laid a snare for me,
Yet I have not gone astray from Your precepts.
I have inherited Your testimonies forever,
For they are the joy of my heart.
I have inclined my heart to perform Your statutes
Forever, even to the end.

Psalm 119:97-112

The Psalmist so loved and appreciated God's law that he dedicated his life to its study and application to his life. When you love God, you love to study His law. This is the second personal sign we can gain from Jesus's statement in John 14:15. When the passion of your heart is to study His Word, the Bible, and the study of His Word and the application of that study to your life brings you great joy, it is a good sign that you love God. Jesus's intended meaning would have included, "If you love Me, you will study My commandments."

It was written of the scribe Ezra:

> Ezra went up from Babylon, and he was a scribe skilled in the law of Moses, which the LORD God of Israel had given; and the king granted him all he requested because ***the hand of the LORD his God was upon him***. Some of the sons of Israel and some of the priests, the Levites, the singers, the gatekeepers and the temple servants went up to Jerusalem in the seventh year of King Artaxerxes.
>
> He came to Jerusalem in the fifth month, which was in the seventh year of the king. For on the first of the first month he began to go up from Babylon; and on the first of the fifth month he came to Jerusalem, ***because the good hand of his God was upon him***. For Ezra had <u>set his heart to study the law of the LORD</u> and <u>to practice it</u>, and <u>to teach His statutes and ordinances in Israel</u> (Ezra 7:6-10).

That passage from Ezra 7 is very interesting because it twice uses the phrase "the good hand of God was upon him." It must be noted, however, there are slight differences in the use. The first reference says the hand of *the Lord* his God was upon him. In the second reference, it only mentions *his God*. In the first reference, the Hebrew word is יְהוָֹה, *Yhvh* (the proper name for God: Jehovah) while in the second, the Hebrew word is אֱלֹהִים, *Elohim*, the plural notation of God. Ezra had the complete blessing and power of the Trinity on his work. With that blessing, Ezra committed to do three distinct tasks: he would study the law, practice the law, and teach the law.

Ezra was a scribe. Scribes spent considerable time copying the law. They copied the law, letter by letter, day after day, reading it, copying it, and reading it again to ensure they copied it correctly. They copied the copy of the scripture and copied it over and over so that they could have some level of retention. Scribes took dictation, took notes, and copied down letters to be sent, tasks that we would call the work of a secretary or an office assistant. That is the level of detail that Ezra had with the law. You might think after days and days of performing these tasks that Ezra might have been tired of reading the law. If it were only Ezra in his own power, he might have felt that way. This passage, however, says that the good hand of God was upon him. This important statement says that this good hand changed the way Ezra looked at his life. Ezra had something inside of him that spurred him to be different, to go above and beyond the normal work of a scribe. He "set his heart" to study the law. That Hebrew word for "set his heart" paints a deep picture of Ezra's commitment. The word is כּוּן, *kun*, which means a fixed determination, a gaze of firm commitment, an unwavering, resilient pursuit of dedication that was so deep a desire that it had an impact on the life and set a direction to a new course. This is the level of commitment that Ezra had.

For a moment, let's just forget what Ezra did with that commitment. Let's examine the motivation for the commitment. Ezra's motivation was from the hand of God on him. It is that same motivation that the Psalmist had.

Do you have that motivation to study Jesus's commandments? Do you feel the hand of God resting upon you such that you lovingly pursue the study of His Word in order to apply it to your life? Is the passion of your heart to learn more of the Bible and what it can teach you? If that passion exists in your life, it is a positive sign that you love God. If you truly love God, you are committed to study the Bible, and you are committed to learn from it. It's a firm determination because you want to hear from the Lord. The Lord speaks to us through His Word. We need communion with His Word.

Surveys show that people who identify as Christians spend a good bit of time studying the Bible. But do you know how much the average Christian spends on a weekly basis in Bible study and prayer? Five hours? Three hours? Would you believe that for survey respondents who identify as Christians, the answer is less than one hour of Bible study a week? Barna conducts some great research into Christian beliefs and practices, and they define "Evangelical Christians" as a separate group from a general "Christian" category. Evangelical

Christians are the most committed to the practice of following Jesus's commandments, not merely holding Christian beliefs. The most committed group of Evangelical Christians report that their individual time in Bible Study is only one hour! Can you believe it? Can you imagine having a love relationship with somebody, perhaps your beloved spouse, and only talking to that person for an hour a week? Only an hour. So, on Valentine's Day, let's say I got up at nine o'clock in the morning and thought to myself, "Well, I'm going to give my spouse a card and spend an hour with her, and then I'm done for the week." Only a one-hour commitment, and I have finished my commitment to her for that week. If I only spent one hour with my bride, and that's all the time I spent interacting with and listening to her in a week, she would probably say that this is not much of a love relationship. It wouldn't be. For some people, though, the only time that they are in the Word to study is on Sunday morning, and that's it.

What do think the Lord's reaction to that level of commitment is?

Obviously, some people do not quite understand that Christians are supposed to be like Ezra, having "set their hearts" and being committed to studying Jesus's commandments. But, if you love the Lord, your motivation for hearing from the Lord is very high, and you will want to study the Bible. It will be a driving passion that excites you.

The first sign that you love God was that you are obeying His commandments. You learn about those commandments through the study of His Word with a dedicated effort. So, these first two signs that you love God work together in tandem.

A subset of David's Psalm 19, verses 7-14, extols the benefits of the law:

> The law of the LORD is **perfect**, restoring the soul;
> The testimony of the LORD is **sure**, making wise the simple.
> The precepts of the LORD are **right**, rejoicing the heart;
> The commandment of the LORD is **pure**, enlightening the eyes.
> The fear of the LORD is **clean**, enduring forever;
> The judgments of the LORD are **true**; they are righteous altogether.
>
> They are more desirable than gold, yes, than much fine gold;
> Sweeter also than honey and the drippings of the honeycomb.
> Moreover, by them Your servant is warned;
> In keeping them, there is great reward.
> Who can discern his errors? Acquit me of hidden faults.
>
> Also keep back Your servant from presumptuous sins;
> Let them not rule over me;
> Then I will be blameless,
> And I shall be acquitted of great transgression.

Let the words of my mouth and the meditation of my heart
Be acceptable in Your sight,
O LORD, my rock and my Redeemer.

The law is "perfect," "sure," "right," "pure," "clean," and "true."

These are undisputed facts.

But what about the benefits of the law? The benefits of having this

Word in front of you and studying it mean that your soul is restored,

you are made wise, your heart is filled with joy, and your eyes are

enlightened. Studying the Bible is guaranteed to bring benefits. If

you study the Bible, then these events will come to pass in your life.

God told Joshua more about these benefits:

> This book of the law shall not depart from your mouth, but
> you shall meditate on it day and night, so that you may be
> careful to do according to all that is written in it; for then
> you will make your way prosperous, and then you will
> have success (Joshua 1:8).

If you want success in life, God promises that you will have it when

you keep the law in view all the days of your life, when you meditate

on it day and night, and when you carefully follow it. I have recently

shared this passage with the youth group at our church. When

young people begin to think about having a successful life, where do

we want them to get the model for that success? Should it be a veteran businessman who has "stepped over many bodies" on the way to the top? Should it be a businesswoman who has compromised her personal values in order to achieve a CEO position in her company? Or, should it be the example of someone like Joshua, who faithfully obeyed God and was commended by God throughout his life for being diligent to His purposes?

Some of our college students at our church are facing this struggle now and are seeking counsel. I know several middle-aged adults who still are trying to figure out who they want to be when they grow up. The Bible is clear on what constitutes a successful life. I counsel young people when they go out into the workforce, and I mentor them as they grow in their professional careers. Many do not know what they want to do when they leave college. Many have no solid foundation. They may have a degree, but they do not have any directional path. To encourage these students as they begin their careers, I meet with them and talk about being a true success in life and in business. The most important message I give them is that my success had very little to do with me. On the other hand, it had everything to do with God and everything to do with my commitment to set my heart to study His Word and to follow His commandments. Success in life is a major benefit of committing yourself to the study of the Bible.

But what is the motivation for the study of the Bible? The motivation is found in Psalm 119. If you look at the words that the Psalmist uses in Psalm 119, you see his motivation for the study of the Word.

Verse	Motivation
14	I have **rejoiced** in the way of Your testimonies
16	I shall **delight** in Your statutes
24	Your testimonies also are **my delight**
55	O LORD, I remember Your name in the night, and keep Your law.
97	**O how I love** Your law! It is my meditation, all the day
119	Therefore **I love** Your testimonies
159	Consider how **I love** Your precepts
162	**I rejoice** at Your word
163	I hate and despise falsehood, But **I love** Your law.
165	**Those who love** Your law have great peace,
167	My soul keeps Your testimonies, and **I love them** exceedingly.

We can see that the Psalmist's view of the Bible is filled with love, rejoicing, and delight. Verse 55 shows us that it is so personal to him that he would remember God's name in the night and long to keep His law. The Word is so personal to him that he owns it.

Some of you on the last Valentine's Day may have gone to your spouse and said, "Oh how I love you!" How many of you have ever uttered a prayer to God and said, "Oh how I love thy law! It is my

43

meditation – all day today"? The Psalmist so loved God's Word that he wrote it down for all eternity to see.

How is your love for the Bible?

Can you join the Psalmist and say that you love the law like that?

A great example of the effect of the law on your life is found in Luke 24:13-35, the story of Jesus's walking after His resurrection along a path out of Jerusalem. Jesus just shows up beside two individuals who are walking a little bit north of Jerusalem on the way to Emmaus.

One of those individuals is Jesus's uncle, Cleopas[4], who would have, no doubt, recognized the Lord. Because Cleopas knows Him, the Lord hides His appearance from these two individuals. Luke records:

> And behold, two of them were going that very day to a
> village named Emmaus, which was about seven miles from
> Jerusalem. And they were talking with each other about all

---

[4] St. Jerome posited that Cleopas was Jesus's uncle in the 4th century writing *Against Heveldius* described by "St Cleophas: Christ's Uncle and Also the Father and Grandfather of 4 Apostles - Taylor Marshall," accessed June 20, 2020, https://taylormarshall.com/2012/04/st-cleophas-christs-uncle-and-also.html. Also see "Icon of Yahshua (Jesus) Breaking Bread with Cleopas in Emmaus by the Hand of Nicholas Papas," accessed June 20, 2020, http://www.biblesearchers.com/hebrewchurch/primitive/primitive16.shtml.

these things which had taken place. While they were talking and discussing, Jesus Himself approached and began traveling with them. But *their eyes were prevented from recognizing Him.*

And He said to them, "What are these words that you are exchanging with one another as you are walking?" And they stood still, looking sad. One of them, named Cleopas, answered and said to Him, "Are You the only one visiting Jerusalem and unaware of the things which have happened here in these days?" And He said to them, "What things?"

And they said to Him, "The things about Jesus the Nazarene, who was a prophet mighty in deed and word in the sight of God and all the people, and how the chief priests and our rulers delivered Him to the sentence of death, and crucified Him.

But we were hoping that it was He who was going to redeem Israel. Indeed, besides all this, it is the third day since these things happened. But, also some women among us amazed us. When they were at the tomb early in the morning, and did not find His body, they came, saying that they had also seen a vision of angels who said that He was alive. Some of those who were with us went to the tomb and found it just exactly as the women also had said; but Him they did not see."

And He said to them, "O foolish men and slow of heart to believe in all that the prophets have spoken! Was it not necessary for the Christ to suffer these things and to enter into His glory?" **Then beginning with Moses and with all the prophets, He explained to them the things concerning Himself in all the Scriptures.**

And they approached the village where they were going, and He acted as though He were going farther. But they urged Him, saying, "Stay with us, for it is getting toward evening, and the day is now nearly over." So, He went in to stay with them. When He had reclined at the table with them, He took the bread and blessed it, and breaking it, He began giving it to them. **Then their eyes were opened, and they recognized Him; and He vanished from their sight.** (Luke 32:13-31)

These two individuals did not know that they were walking next to Jesus, the risen Messiah of Israel. Only when Jesus took the bread and blessed it, performing the exact tasks as He did at the first Lord's Supper (John 13), did they recognize Him. These two individuals were expecting the Messiah to come and restore Israel to glory as her King – in their time frame. They, among many others, wanted this restoration to happen immediately. God's plan had a different timing for those events. Jesus calls them foolish because the Old Testament clearly recorded the story of the Messiah. Then, one of the greatest teaching events ever recorded in the Bible occurs. The risen King, the Messiah of Israel, taught these two individuals His personal story by beginning with Moses and the Prophets, explaining everything to them about God's plan. Wow! Wouldn't YOU have loved to be on that road able to listen to that explanation? Jesus went through the entire Old Testament explaining about Himself and instructing who He was, how He had to die for Israel and the world outside of Israel, and the reason why He had to die for them. Then, they go in and sit down to dinner, and what happens to Jesus? He vanishes, and their eyes are opened to understand what just happened. They were in the Divine Seminary, instructed by the Messiah Himself.

What was their reaction to this event?

> They said to one another, "***Were not our hearts burning within us while He was speaking to us on the road, while He was explaining the Scriptures to us?***"
>
> And they got up that very hour and returned to Jerusalem and found gathered together the eleven and those who were with them, saying, "The Lord has really risen and has appeared to Simon." They began to relate their experiences on the road and how He was recognized by them in the breaking of the bread (Luke 24:32-35).

What did they say after they realize that was Jesus Christ with them?

"Were not our hearts burning within us while He was speaking to us on the road?" They were hearing the very words of Jesus, explaining the Scriptures to them! Their reaction was a burning desire to hear these words and to understand them and to learn more from Him. It was a passionate, burning desire.

Does your heart burn when you hear the words of Jesus explained to you?

Is this the effect that the preached Word has on you?

If the preached Word affects you in this way, then it is a positive sign that you love the Lord. Our hearts should burn when we have the Words of Life spoken to us. We should always be affected by hearing the gospel preached to us. We should never cease to want to hear it, to want to have it explained to us, to long for the deep study of the Word. If the preached Word affects you in this way, it is only because of His influence in your life. Burning desire to know does not come unless He is impacting your life and He is in your life.

If you do not love to hear the Word preached to you, then you should have some concern about your commitment to God. If you believe you are a Christian, but going to church to hear the preaching of the Bible is tedious to you, or if you see it as a burden to you or as something you have to endure, then I would be very concerned about your salvation. This moment may be the time for you to ask yourself, "Why do I feel this way?"

We all can agree that no preacher is perfect, and no one delivers perfect messages on Sunday morning. Most preachers stepping in the pulpit, however, are committed to communicate the Word of God in its full and complete glory to people with the best of their abilities. Those who come to church to listen should quickly forgive the incidental error and treasure the hearing of the Word explained. The writer of Hebrews noted that "the word of God is living and active and sharper than any two-edged sword and piercing as far as the division of soul and spirit, of both joints and marrow, and able to judge the thoughts and intentions of the heart" (Hebrews 4:12). God's Word, spoken to us, is powerful, living, and active in our lives even if the preacher's chosen prose on that day is not "perfect."

If you find yourself overly critical of your Pastor's preaching on Sunday or if you are easily distracted from the message, it might be a sign to you that something is amiss in your Christian life. If you love to hear the Word of God preached to you though, and you long to hear it and to apply its teaching to your life, it is a positive sign that you love God.

Sign #3 – The Support of His Church

The Apostle Peter was an inquisitive man. He was continually bringing questions to the Lord from the Twelve as the spokesman for the group. We are not always sure if they were personal questions from Peter or questions subtly submitted from another disciple for Peter to repeat. Peter was not the only one who asked questions, however. Sometimes, the Lord asked questions to the Twelve, and Peter responded for the group. In one case particularly, Peter's response was a revelation from above.

> Now when Jesus came into the district of Caesarea Philippi, He was asking His disciples, "Who do people say that the Son of Man is?" And they said, "Some say John the Baptist; and others, Elijah; but still others, Jeremiah, or one of the prophets."
>
> He said to them, "But who do you say that I am?"
>
> Simon Peter answered, "You are the Christ, the Son of the living God." And Jesus said to him, "Blessed are you, Simon Barjona, because **flesh and blood did not reveal this to you, but My Father who is in heaven.** I also say to you that you are Peter, and **upon this rock I will build My church; and the gates of Hades will not overpower it"** (Matthew 16:13-18).

When Jesus came into Galilee to begin His ministry, He caused quite a stir among the people. His miracles generated a wide following and popularity from the masses. The people wanted to know who the Man was who was performing all of these miracles. Jesus sought to take this question head on with the Twelve, asking them, "Who do people say that I am?" The Twelve responded with what they had heard from people as they walked along with Jesus in ministry.

Jesus, however, wanted to know what the Twelve thought. "Who do YOU say that I am?" Jesus asked them. There are moments when you can, hypothetically, see Peter surveying the group, collecting responses, and then slowly rising to respond for the Twelve. This moment, however, most likely involved a more immediate standing to attention and confidently announcing a response. Peter announced to Jesus and the Twelve, "You are the Christ!" You can almost hear Peter shouting "You are not only the Son of God, but You are the long-awaited Messiah of Israel." Jesus knows that the only way Peter is going to grasp this fact is if God, the Father, shared this information with him. It is a moment of great importance both to Jesus and the Twelve. They may have had lingering doubts about who Jesus truly was but not after this statement. They knew!

The next statement from Jesus is of equal importance: "I say to you that you are Peter; and upon this rock I will build My church!" This verse has generated much discussion over the centuries. What did Jesus mean about Peter in particular? Jesus is definitely speaking directly to Peter, but when He says, "upon this rock," Jesus is using a feminine reference, not a masculine one. Jesus is not anointing Peter as the foundation of His Church[5], but Jesus is saying that a statement from one who <u>knows</u> that He is the Christ, the Messiah of Israel, IS a foundational element of being IN the Church. The Church is made up of the called-out ones, those whom God has chosen to believe in Jesus and those who would recognize and tell the world that He is the Messiah. The knowledge of that fact, and the acceptance of that fact, can only come from God the Father. Peter became the first Christian, who came to know that Jesus is the Son of God, and he communicated that knowledge to the world. We, likewise, should know that truth and communicate that fact to the world around us.

What does this commitment have to do with our love for God? Jesus promises to build His Church. He continues to build His Church

---

[5] "The Church," The author's intended use of "the Church" is in its most global sense, the Church universal, which consists of local churches as well as all extended ministries with Jesus's mission as their shared goal.

through His people because the Church IS made up of His people. We ARE the Church!

Paul gave us Jesus's plan in his epistle to the Ephesians:

> And He gave some as apostles, and some as prophets, and some as evangelists, and some as pastors and teachers, for the equipping of the saints for the work of service, **to the building up of the body of Christ;** until we all attain to the unity of the faith, and of the knowledge of the Son of God, to a mature man, to the measure of the stature which belongs to the fullness of Christ (Ephesians 4:11-13).

In Ephesians 4, Paul is writing about Jesus's ascension on high after His resurrection. After that event Jesus gave His Church apostles, prophets, evangelists, pastors, and teachers specifically for building up His Church. And, if we love God, we will be part of that building of the Church. It was the passion of Jesus to build His Church; it should also be the passion of His people.

Further, Jesus's last words on earth before His ascension were recorded in Matthew 28. Jesus called His disciples back to Galilee, and Matthew records:

> The eleven disciples proceeded to Galilee, to the mountain which Jesus had designated. When they saw Him, they worshiped Him; but some were doubtful. And Jesus came up and spoke to them, saying, 'All authority has been given

to Me in heaven and on earth. *Go therefore and make disciples of all the nations, baptizing them in the name of the Father and the Son and the Holy Spirit,* **teaching them to observe all that I commanded you***; and lo, I am with you always, even to the end of the age.'*

With Judas gone, the eleven remaining disciples return to Galilee where the risen Jesus meets them and informs them that all authority is now His, both in heaven and on the earth. The disciples have given their very lives to follow Him for three years. They are prepared. There is only one remaining task for them to carry out: they are to make disciples of all the nations. How are they do that? They are to teach the nations to observe all that Jesus commanded them to do. Simply put, they are to pass along the training they received from Jesus to others and to call them to observe those commandments in their lives. Because, Jesus said, "if you love Me, you will obey my commandments!" (John 14:15). If you are teaching others to love Jesus, then you will teach them to obey His commandments. Therefore, if you love God, you will support the building of His Church. If you love God, you will give yourself in service to His Church. The product of love is giving.

Jesus gave this example in the Sermon on the Mount:

Ask, and it will be given to you; seek, and you will find; knock, and it will be opened to you. For everyone who asks receives, and he who seeks finds, and to him who knocks it will be opened. **Or what man is there among you who, when his son asks for a loaf, will give him a stone?** Or if he asks for a fish, he will not give him a snake, will he? If you then, being evil, know how to give good gifts to your children, how much more will your Father who is in heaven give what is good to those who ask Him!

When you love your children, and your children ask for a load of bread, you are not going to give them a stone, are you? If they ask for a fish, you are not going to give them a snake! When you love, you naturally give. Jesus gives those examples to show that the Father's love for His children is the same, and the Father will give good gifts to His own because He loves them.

If you love God, you will give of yourself and what you have to His Church.

In the book of Romans, Paul has, in effect, written his version of the gospel. The first eleven chapters of Romans contain solid teaching. The book contains sound doctrine. It is everything Paul knows about the gospel. In chapter twelve, however, Paul's tone has changed. He is no longer explaining the deep truths of God. Instead, Paul gets personal with his audience, writing:

Therefore, I urge you brethren, by the mercies of God, **to present your bodies a living and holy sacrifice, acceptable**

to God, which is your spiritual service of worship. And do not be conformed to this world, but be transformed by the renewing of your mind, so that you may prove what the will of God is, that which is good and acceptable and perfect (Romans 12:1-2).

In other words, Paul says, "All that I have covered in the first eleven chapters where I have told you how blessed we are in Jesus and how blessed we are to have been called by God to be part of His Church, I have reminded you that we have been rescued from death and brought into life. We have been called out of the world with a special, precious gift. Knowing this, I urge you, I exhort you, and I encourage you to present your bodies as a living and holy sacrifice in service to God, service that will be acceptable to God. It is your calling if you love Him."

The book of Romans is written to both Jews and Gentiles. Paul goes back and forth, addressing both groups, throughout the book. Chapters nine through eleven were written specifically to the Jews in Rome, a group who would know a lot about what a holy sacrifice was since they grew up with the sacrificial system. To give your bodies as a spiritual sacrifice WAS to bring worship to God. Paul writes that, while the form of sacrifice has changed, sacrifice is still required: you do not sacrifice animals any longer; you give your body as a living and holy sacrifice, your spiritual worship.

The first event that should happen in your life, after you come to Jesus in faith, is that you should give of your time in service to His Church. If you love Him, that is.

The giving of your body in sacrificial service has several manifestations. If you look at the word "sacrifice," what is your first thought? What does sacrifice mean to you? What event in the Bible do you think of where sacrifice is displayed? Most of us would think about Jesus on the cross as the primary example. Paul is not writing about that level of sacrifice, though.

Is there an event in your own life that comes to mind where you sacrificed for someone else or where another individual sacrificed for you?

I remember a time when I was having lunch with a Muslim named Rif in a cafe in downtown Atlanta. I was trying to explain what Jesus Christ sacrificed for us. Rif would have none of it. He didn't want to listen. He did not understand what Jesus's sacrifice meant for him because he had no personal reference or example. I understand that as I had that same lack of example in my past. To understand the true meaning of sacrifice, we need an example. So, I gave him one.

I said, "Rif, let's say your wife is walking outside on this street," as I pointed to the road outside the cafe. "Let's say I look up now, and I see a truck is going toward your wife as she's walking across the street with the baby carriage and your two kids age two and three in tow."

"I am inside the restaurant, but I see that your wife does not see the car. I jump out of my seat, run out there, and push her out of the way. She is safe and sitting on the curb, but that truck that was going to hit her, hit me instead, and I perished in the accident."

"The truck killed me. It's a sacrifice. I have sacrificed my life for your wife and your two kids. Does this mean anything to you?"

I could see Rif struggling with that thought for a while, and then he said, "You know, I would have to repay your family for that. I would have to do something for your family because you did something for me."

I said, "Rif, I am a single man. I have no kids. I have no brothers and sisters since I was an only child. And, you know, my parents died years ago."

I am doing a really good job with him, right? I am giving him no out. There is no answer for him.

So, what does he say? He says, "Then I will hate you!"

"You will hate me?" I said. "What do you mean you will hate me? I just gave my life for your wife and kids! Why would you hate me?"

Rif looked at me confidently and said, "Because I would have no way to repay what you have done for me. There would be no way to return the sacrifice."

I said, "Thank you, Rif, you have just proved my point. There is no way repay His sacrifice for you." And I was able to talk to Rif using the Bible verses about sacrifice and what Jesus's sacrifice for us was all about. There is no repayment but we should simply love Him for His sacrifice.

What story of sacrifice comes to your mind? I think of Abraham and Isaac that I mentioned earlier. There was a little cartoon video when our kids were young. We put them in front of the television, and they saw Isaac bringing up the wood saying, "I'm coming along, Dad." Isaac is going up there. He's got the wood in his arms and has no idea what's going to happen. Abraham says, "We have to go to this mountain top on Mount Moriah, Son. Guess what's going to happen? When we get up there, you are the sacrifice!"

Another story of sacrifice that comes to mind is the time Jesus was sitting with the disciples at the temple, and they are observing the treasury. They watch various people coming to bring offerings there, and a Pharisee comes up, and he's got a big pile of money. It is all in individual coins because the treasury is a coin case in front of the Temple. Any coin put into the treasury box is going to make a noise. Ping. Pang. Pong. Do you know what the Pharisees would do? They would change their larger denomination coins into the smallest denomination possible, so they had more coins. In our monetary system, changing a $100 bill into pennies would be the equivalent action. They would go to all that trouble so they could go up to the treasury box and insert all coins in over a long period of time. Everybody's attention is drawn to the noise. And then the Pharisees would stand in front of the treasury and orate a big prayer in the middle of the temple area.

The disciples and Jesus are watching scenes like that as Luke notes (Luke 20:45-47). And then this little old widowed lady comes up. Perhaps she was walking slowly, not drawing much attention. You could imagine Jesus nudging Peter to look at her. Luke records the scene:

> And He looked up and saw the rich putting their gifts into the treasury. And He saw a poor widow putting in two small copper coins. And He said, '**Truly I say to you, this poor widow put in more than all of them; for they all out of their surplus put into the offering; but she out of her poverty put in all that she had to live on.'**

Jesus says that this widow gave more than everybody else. She gave out of her poverty, not out of her excess. Out of her poverty she gave: sacrifice. Those rich people did not give out of their poverty. The widow did not have anything except those two small coins to live on. That is a definition of sacrifice to me.

What about you? What is your definition of sacrifice?

So, I realized I needed to consult the most powerful Oracle I know in today's world, so I held up my phone and asked the question, "Hey, Siri, what does sacrifice mean? Siri responded, "An act of slaughtering an animal, person, or possession as an offering to a deity or Christ's offering of Himself at the crucifixion." Wow. Even Siri knows about the sacrifice of Jesus Christ! That definition is surely going to change if some atheists find out about this response and Siri will no longer be able to answer that way. Sacrifice is an active giving up of something valued for the sake of someone else. It is worthy to give up something valued for the sake of another, like giving up your time to do some task for somebody who needs assistance. This is what the world thinks sacrifice means.

It is a Saturday morning, and you have worked hard all week. You are tired, but you know that the church office has announced that a workday is scheduled on that day to clean the church or to beautify the grounds. You could stay at home, sleep in, read a book, or maybe even go out to a nice brunch with family. Or you could go to the workday at the church. You can sacrifice what you wanted to do for that day, and you could come to the church and work to beautify the property.

Perhaps you have been notified that there is a member of the church who is struggling with household chores since her husband passed away last year. The house is not being cared for as it was before, and the widow needs someone to come and assist her with basic repairs. Maybe a member of the church has lost a job and does not have the financial means to sustain his house for a period of time. You can sacrifice some of your groceries and deliver or, better yet, offer to prepare a meal to help.

There may be a place of service where the church needs a role to be filled. Let's say the children's ministry leader needs a couple to teach a Sunday School class for three to five-year old children or to sit with young babies for an hour during the worship service. The former might require you to miss attending your Sunday School class or to get up an hour earlier each Sunday for a season. The latter would require one weekend out of the month where you could not attend the worship service with your family.

In each of these situations, you should say to yourself, "Why not me?" If this is your heart, to serve the body of Christ and build it up, it's a positive sign that you love God because you long to give yourself in service to Him and assist in building His church.

If you love God, you will also financially support His church. You will give to his Church. Those who love God give because the product of love is giving, right? What might financial giving to your church entail? Maybe you skip a trip to Starbucks one day a week. I have no idea what a cup of Starbucks coffee costs right now. Let's say it is five dollars, and you love your Starbucks coffee each morning. It gets you going! But if you skip Starbucks each workday for a week, that is twenty-five dollars for a week, one hundred dollars for the month! Instead of spending that money on yourself, you give that one hundred dollars to a missionary. You are sacrificing what you would like to have or what you would like to do for another cause – something more worthy – to build His Church.

This is basic sacrificial giving. There is a beautiful passage in 2nd Corinthians, chapter 8, where Paul writes about sacrificial giving.

> Now, brethren, we wish to make known to you the grace of God which has been given in the churches of Macedonia, that **in a great ordeal of affliction their abundance of joy and their deep poverty overflowed** in the wealth of their liberality. For I testify that according to their ability, and beyond their ability, **they gave of their own accord, begging us with much urging for the favor of participation in the support of the saints**, and this, not as we had expected, but they first gave themselves to the Lord and to us by the will of God (2 Corinthians 8:1-5).

Paul writes to the Corinthian church that another group of people, the churches in Macedonia, demanded to give to the support of the saints in Jerusalem who were suffering under the persecution of the Romans. Not only did they demand to participate in the offering, but they did so when they, themselves, were in great poverty and affliction. They had so little themselves, but they wanted to give to support others. You do not make such a sacrifice unless you have the love of God in you. Can you imagine that scene of the widow with two small coins going to the treasury and saying, "Well, I only have two small coins. That's not very much. It's not going to help anyone, really. I might as well just keep it for myself and buy some food." What would YOU have done in her situation? Like the widow, the Macedonian Christians made the decision to help others.

The Apostle Paul sent a letter to a group of believers in Philippi and wrote this:

> Therefore if there is any encouragement in Christ, if there is any consolation of love, if there is any fellowship of the Spirit, if any affection and compassion, **make my joy complete** by being of the same mind, maintaining the same love, united in spirit, intent on one purpose. Do nothing from selfishness or empty conceit, **but with humility of mind regard one another as more important than yourselves; do not merely look out for your own personal interests, but also for the interests of others** (Philippians 2:1-4).

Paul loved this group of believers in Philippi. In the first chapter of Philippians, the first eleven verses call out his thoughts about the new church:

> **I thank my God in all my remembrance of you**, always offering prayer with joy in my every prayer for you all, in view of your participation in the gospel from the first day until now. For I am confident of this very thing, that He who began a good work in you will perfect it until the day of Christ Jesus.

For it is only right for me to feel this way about you all, because *I have you in my heart*, since both in my imprisonment and in the defense and confirmation of the gospel, you all are partakers of grace with me. **For God is my witness, how I long for you all with the affection of Christ Jesus.**

And this I pray, that your love may abound still more and more in real knowledge and all discernment, so that you may approve the things that are excellent, in order to be sincere and blameless until the day of Christ; having been filled with the fruit of righteousness which [comes] through Jesus Christ, to the glory and praise of God (Philippians 1:3-11).

Paul thanked God for them. He viewed this church as some of his children. He prayed for them, wept to God for them, and loved them deeply. He longed to be with them and was concerned for the church's very existence since Paul was in prison and unable to visit. One of his prayers for them was their love would abound more and more and that they would continue to show great love "in real knowledge and all discernment."

What is this real knowledge? It extends beyond simply having the facts. A Greek preposition in the original language intensifies this knowledge. Real knowledge is knowledge gained through "first-hand relationship." It is "contact-knowledge" that is appropriate to "first-hand, or experiential knowing." It is not just understanding but placing into practice the knowledge that was received. It is living out what you have been taught to do and personally experiencing it. Paul is praying that the love of Christ that they have been taught would be acted upon by the Philippian Christians such that they would have personal experience with sharing it. Paul also had great love for another church as he writes at the beginning of his first letter to the Thessalonians:

> **We give thanks to God always for all of you**, making mention of you in our prayers; constantly bearing in mind your work of faith and labor of love and steadfastness of hope in our Lord Jesus Christ in the presence of our God and Father, knowing, brethren beloved by God, His choice of you; for our gospel did not come to you in word only, **but also in power and in the Holy Spirit and with full conviction**; just as you know what kind of men we proved to be among you for your sake.
>
> **You also became imitators of us and of the Lord**, having received the word in much tribulation with the joy of the Holy Spirit, so that you became an example to all the believers in Macedonia and in Achaia.
>
> **For the word of the Lord has sounded forth from you**, not only in Macedonia and Achaia, but also in every place your faith toward God has gone forth, **so that we have no need to say anything** (1 Thessalonians 1:2-8).

Paul loved these believers and prayed for them. These men and women received not only the words of the gospel, but knowledge was amplified in the power of the Holy Spirit with full conviction, meaning that they received an effectual calling to faith. It changed their lives. They became imitators of not only Paul and his cohorts but also of the Lord Himself. What a commendation from Paul to this young church! The change in the Thessalonians' lives was so demonstrative that the word of the Lord sounded forth from them. People in the surrounding area knew about this little church because its members were living out the gospel toward others. They were showing the love of Christ to their community. They were living so graciously that Paul did not need to say anything else to them!

Seriously? Can you imagine your pastor coming up to preach on Sunday morning and saying, "You guys are doing EVERYTHING well. I do not need to give you any further commands. You are living out the gospel to everyone so that everyone in our city knows who we are. It's amazing!"

Why are the Philippian and Thessalonian churches examples of sacrificial giving? Both churches were in Macedonia, and Thessalonika was the capital of the Roman province. When Paul writes to the Corinthians speaking of the Christians in Macedonia, he wrote:

> Now, brethren, we wish to make known to you the grace of God **which has been given in the churches of**

Macedonia, that in a great ordeal of affliction their abundance of joy and their deep poverty overflowed in the wealth of their liberality (2 Corinthians 8:1-2).

Paul's prayer that the love in the church in Philippi "may abound still more and more in real knowledge and all discernment" was answered by God. They experienced the love of sharing what they had with others; despite their poverty, they were "begging" to be able to give because they loved God. Amazing love!

Can you say that you are motivated to give like that? If you do, it is a positive sign that you love God.

In the very next chapter in Paul's epistle to the Corinthians, he writes in (2 Corinthians 9:1-5):

> For **it is superfluous for me to write to you about this ministry to the saints**; for I know your readiness, of which I boast about you to the Macedonians, namely, that Achaia has been prepared since last year, and your zeal has stirred up most of them. But I have sent the brethren, **in order that our boasting about you may not be made empty in this case, so that, as I was saying, you may be prepared**; otherwise if any Macedonians come with me and find you unprepared, we-- not to speak of you-- will be put to shame by this confidence. So, **I thought it necessary to urge the brethren that they would go on ahead to you and arrange beforehand your previously promised**

bountiful gift, so that the same would be ready as a bountiful gift and not affected by covetousness.

Paul writes that he has no doubt that the Corinthians will contribute to the saints in need in Jerusalem. He knows they will be ready because he knows that they have been an example to the Macedonian churches. Their example is the way encouragement normally works. When you hear of someone performing an amazing work for the Lord, doesn't it spur your desire to do the same? When a sister church is supporting a specific ministry, does it not encourage your church to do likewise? Christianity is a brotherhood and a sisterhood where iron does sharpen iron (Proverbs 27:17), and each of us will be encouraged to step up in commitment and service through the visible example of others.

Paul, however, wants to make sure that they are prepared to give – ahead of time. Some planning needs to be involved when you give to support the Lord's Church. Some of our giving may be spontaneous, such as the support for new ministry opportunities, but most of our giving should be a planned well in advance. Why? Paul answers that question. Because in the moment believers could be affected by momentary covetousness. In the moment when the offering plate goes by (for those of you in churches that pass the plate around on Sunday mornings), your hands might not deliver the donation into the plate. Perhaps you remember that you do not have any checks with you or that you do not have the correct denomination of bills that you want to give. All sorts of "in the moment" excuses could come into your head when it is time to give. We can all be moved by momentary lapses in concentration and fail to respond in the way we might want had we planned ahead of time.

The point Paul is making is important, and his motivation is not to ensure that the ministry to the saints in Jerusalem is met. He knows that the Lord is in charge of all of these ministries. He knows the needs will be met, exactly as the saints in Jerusalem need them to be. Does he want to bring the offering to them? Yes. But that is not his primary concern in writing to the Corinthians. His motivation for writing is that the Corinthians would experience personal remorse if they do not respond to the opportunity to give at the appropriate time. If the offering plate passes by you, and you do not give anything, do you feel guilty afterward? Do you wish that you had given, and do you emotionally punish yourself for that lack of response? Yes! It happens to all of us from time to time. Paul does not want the Corinthian believers to experience that regret but instead to experience the joy of giving just as was experienced by the Macedonian Christians.

Paul also highlighted this same point to the Philippians:

> You yourselves also know, Philippians, that at the first preaching of the gospel, after I left Macedonia, no church shared with me in the matter of giving and receiving but you alone; for even in Thessalonica you sent a gift more than once for my needs. **Not that I seek the gift itself**, **but I seek for the profit which increases to your account.**

> But I have received everything in full and have an abundance; I am amply supplied, having received from Epaphroditus what you have sent, a fragrant aroma, an acceptable sacrifice, well-pleasing to God. And **my God will supply all your needs according to His riches in glory in Christ Jesus** (Philippians 4:15-20).

Paul knew that the needs of the church in Jerusalem would be met because he trusted in God's provision. God always met Paul's needs so there was no doubt in Paul's mind about God's meeting the needs of the Jerusalem saints. Therefore, Paul confidently wrote to the Philippians that God would supply THEIR needs according to the riches of Christ Jesus. Paul was seeking the individual profit and benefit of each Philippian giver since their giving would be attributed to their individual account.

So, Paul reminds them that they promised to support the saints in Jerusalem, and he was coming to receive the offering. Has asked them to be ready – for their own sakes. So that they would not fail at the appropriate time and experience remorse, they needed to be prepared to give.

Next, Paul writes:

> Now this I say, **he who sows sparingly will also reap sparingly, and he who sows bountifully will also reap bountifully**. Each one must do just as he has purposed in his heart, not grudgingly or under compulsion, **for God loves a cheerful giver.**
>
> And **God is able to make all grace abound to you, so that always having all sufficiency in everything, you may have an abundance for every good deed** (2 Corinthians 9:6-8).

Paul encourages them to give and writes, "He who sows sparingly shall also reap sparingly, and he who sows bountifully will also reap bountifully." That is the benefit of giving: its reward. The more one sows, the more one reaps. God shows us the effect of giving to the donor. There is a condition to that giving, however. The believer's benefit for giving is a reward based on the reason FOR the giving. Paul writes that "each one must do just as he has purposed in his heart" but "not grudgingly or under compulsion." Why?

I can write a lot about the benefit of giving. I can write about "if you sow sparingly, you reap sparingly." I can mention that "it is better to give than to receive" (Acts 20:35). I can discuss the greater the gifts that we give, the more abundant the Lord makes our life. When I teach from these verses, I am speaking about the full benefits of giving. A secondary purpose of this book is for believers to understand the benefits of our life in Christ when we follow His commandments, yes, but the main purpose of the book is the central motivation for following. In this example, there is a love aspect in giving. If you love Him, you will support His Church.

The motivation is found in the next verse: God loves a cheerful giver! If giving to your church comes from a position of requirement, your church will receive a benefit, but you, please hear me, will have no reward from God. Many churches have pastors who teach this section of Corinthians with incorrect motives and instruct their congregations to have those same incorrect motives. The thrust of their teaching is that if a person gives to God, God is almost required to return it back to that person. God becomes a proverbial Genie in the Bottle! No, that is not how it works in God's economy. God's people are cheerful givers. They give out of a love for Him and His church, pure and simple. Many times when I am in church, I overhear comments during the passing of the offering plate and simply shake my head. I once overheard a husband and wife arguing about the amount of the contribution, and finally the husband said, "Fine. Do it. I don't care!" followed by the crossing of his arms in disagreement. I walked away from that situation after the service saying to myself, "God will give no reward for that gift to the husband." He had totally missed the point of giving to God.

God has all the cattle on a thousand hills (Psalm 50:10)! He does not need our money. He gives us monies as a gift and an outpouring of His love. If you think about it, what possession do you have that is not a result of something being given to you? "Well, I earned money at my job and bought this new car!" Yes, you probably did. Someone offered you that job, right? You worked, but the job was provided by someone else. As I tell my brothers and sisters in our church, even your name was gifted to you. Nothing you can claim was received on your own without the assistance or beneficial gift of someone else. Your education, your personal possessions, your children, your knowledge, and your very name have all been gifted to you. Everything is His.

What He wants to see is your willing sharing of those gifts with others. To encourage the Corinthians even more, Paul writes that God is able to make all grace abound to them. He owns all the wealth on the planet, and He can move it wherever He wants to move it. When you have the proper motivation for giving, God will bestow His grace upon you "so that always having all sufficiency in everything, you may have an abundance for every good deed." In other words, Paul is saying that God will meet your needs. Not only that, but you will have an abundance for every opportunity to give in the future. Why? Because if God knows that what He gives you will flow out to support His Church, He will continue to give to you so that you can continue to support His work. It's a continual flow. Referring back to the commitment of Abraham to sacrifice his only son, Isaac, God said, "Now I KNOW that you fear [love] Me" (Genesis 22:12). When God knows that you are a cheerful giver, you will be [cheerfully] rewarded BY God. God will cheerfully give to you!

If you were to attribute cheerfulness to an organ in your body, what organ would that be? Would it be your mind? Would it be your stomach? Would it be your skin?

The Bible notes that cheerfulness is a condition of the heart:

A glad heart makes a cheerful face (Proverbs 15:13).

All the days of the afflicted are evil, but the cheerful of heart has a continual feast (Proverbs 15:15).

A cheerful heart is good medicine, but a crushed spirit dries up the bones (Proverbs 17:22).

Rejoice, O young man, in your youth, and let your heart
cheer you in the days of your youth (Ecclesiastes 11:9).

When you give to your church, is it a mental exercise or is it a heart exercise? Are you calculating percentages of income or asking the Lord, "What should I give this week or this month?" What does your heart tell you about giving when you purpose in your heart to give?

What Paul is writing to the Corinthians is that there is a difference between giving in the old system and giving in the new system. In the Jewish sacrificial system giving was a mental exercise because you were following the law, and the law was clear about percentages and requirements. Yes, there were freewill offerings in the Jewish system, but these offerings still had specific items and quantities mentioned. In the new system, giving is meant to be a heart exercise with a heartfelt motivation. You see it in different places in the Bible, but Paul really highlights this principle for the Corinthian believers.

For much of my work life prior to entering the ministry, I had my own business preparing taxes for my clients. I still have a few clients, many of them pastors, for whom I still prepare taxes. When I put together a tax return, I am looking at a person's income. I am looking at their charitable contributions. I can gather a great amount of information about individuals from looking at their tax returns. One of my clients used to work for a large conglomerate. He had a C-Level position in a media company making all sorts of money each year: $600,000 one year, $700,000 the next year, $800,000 the year after that. I would look at his charitable contributions for each of those years and only find $1,000 or $2,000 in contributions. For someone given so much, to give so little is just flabbergasting. My first thought is that this guy certainly does not love God. I don't know whom he loves, but his love for God is not where mine would be if I were in that situation. If only I could have been a little voice whispering in his ear and prompting him to give more from his heart.

Let me contrast him with another one of my clients, a man who joined me in prison ministry for several years. He was an athlete, and after I had been in prison ministry with him for a little bit, he found out that I prepared taxes. I can remember a distinct conversation we had in the prison yard one day where he was railing against the IRS for thirty minutes. I was used to hearing people railing about the IRS, and I've probably heard every story under the sun about people's issues with the IRS. He said, "Geoffrey, I make $48,000 a year. Can you tell me why I cannot give more than $24,000 and deduct it?" I must admit that I was a little shocked. He continued, "That's a stupid limitation. The IRS is telling me that I have to limit my deductions to $24,000. I can't give any more than 50 percent of my income." That was the first time I ever heard that complaint in my long tax preparation career. It impacted me because he had a great perspective. I was willing to give him more of <u>our</u> family funds simply so he could give more money to support the Lord's ministry! His example showed the heartfelt motivation to give and the kind of attitude you want to see from God's people.

I also participated in financial planning with my clients including the construction of family budgets. Many clients and some of our church members have asked me what percentage of income should be given to the church and if they should give a standard ten percent.

My response is to answer with a question:

Do you want to live under the **law**, or do you want to live under **grace**?

More often than not, I get a very quizzical look from them. I tell them that it is our choice what we give. We are not compelled by any specific percentage in the Bible because the old system under Moses does not apply to Christians.

In the Old Testament Jewish system, three giving events each required a tithe or ten percent of one's income for the year.

80

There was a ten percent annual tithe that was called the Levite Tithe:

> **To the sons of Levi**, behold, **I have given all the tithe in Israel for an inheritance**, in return for their service which they perform, the service of the tent of meeting. The sons of Israel shall not come near the tent of meeting again, or they will bear sin and die. Only the Levites shall perform the service of the tent of meeting, and they shall bear their iniquity; it shall be a perpetual statute throughout your generations, and among the sons of Israel they shall have no inheritance. **For the tithe of the sons of Israel, which they offer as an offering to the LORD, I have given to the Levites for an inheritance** (Numbers 18:21-26).

The Levites were not given any land as an inheritance among the tribes of Israel since they were to be in service to the other tribes and to God. The Levites were a tribe of priests, and they were not called to have a field of crops or to tend livestock. They were to be dedicated to the service of God in His temple. Because of this commitment to His service and the Levites' lack of inheritance, they were to be supported by the other tribes with a ten percent tithe granted to them from all the income of Israel.

There was also a ten percent annual tithe called the Festival Tithe:

> You shall surely tithe all the produce from what you sow, which comes out of the field every year. **You shall eat in the presence of the LORD your God, at the place where He chooses to establish His name**, the tithe of your grain,

your new wine, your oil, and the firstborn of your herd and your flock, **so that you may learn to fear [love] the LORD your God always.**

If the distance is so great for you that you are not able to bring the tithe, since the place where the LORD your God chooses to set His name is too far away from you when the LORD your God blesses you, then you shall **exchange it for money**, and bind the money in your hand and go to the place which the LORD your God chooses.

You may spend the money **for whatever your heart desires**: for oxen, or sheep, or wine, or strong drink, or whatever your heart desires; and there you shall eat in the presence of the LORD your God and rejoice, you and your household (Deuteronomy 14:22-26).

This tithe was different than the Levite Tithe. It was another ten percent that was meant to be brought to the closest town for celebrations and national feasts so that Israel would recognize and celebrate God's kind grace among them. Note that if the people lived so far away from the place of celebration, they could exchange cattle or produce for money and then bring the money in order to help pay for the festival elements. The festival elements could be anything their heart desired: oxen, sheep, wine, or even strong drink! These festival elements were to create a massive party, celebrating Israel's love for God.

In the next verse after this passage, God repeats His call for the Levite Tithe, noting that the people should not neglect the Levites among them:

> Also, you shall not neglect the Levite who is in your town, for he has no portion or inheritance among you (Deuteronomy 22:27).

Lastly, there was a required tithe called the Poor or Welfare Tithe:

> At the **end of every third year you shall bring out all the tithe of your produce in that year and shall deposit it in your town.** The Levite, because he has no portion or inheritance among you, and the alien, the orphan and the widow who are in your town, shall come and eat and be satisfied, in order that the LORD your God may bless you in all the work of your hand which you do (Deuteronomy 22:28-29).

This third required tithe was not an annual tithe but was one required to be given every third year: three and a third percent every year. This tithe was to be brought into the town and deposited in a storehouse for future welfare needs of the poor, the foreigner or alien, the orphan, and the widow who could not provide for themselves. In addition to this required tithe, those who owned fields were to leave the corners of the field unharvested so that the poor could come and glean part of the harvest (Leviticus 19:9; 23:22).

This gleaning is referenced in the book of Ruth where she, a foreigner, gathered at the fields of Boaz (Ruth 2:23).

It is the Welfare Tithe that the prophet Malachi wrote about:

> "Will a man rob God? Yet you are robbing Me! But you say, 'How have we robbed You?' In tithes and offerings. You are cursed with a curse, for you are robbing Me, the whole nation of you!
>
> Bring the whole tithe into the storehouse, so that there may be food in My house, and test Me now in this," says the LORD of hosts, "if I will not open for you the windows of heaven and pour out for you a blessing until it overflows" (Malachi 3:8-10).

The people were not following God's command concerning the tithe and caring for the welfare of others. This Welfare Tithe was the only one that was to be brought into a storehouse for future needs. How often have you heard an entire sermon based on Malachi 3:8-10 where the preacher is pounding the pulpit talking about giving to the church? Those messages, while probably well-intentioned, unfortunately miss the mark as the prophet is only referencing a single of the three required tithes.

So, there is a ten percent for the Levite Tithe, another ten percent required for the Festival Tithe, and, finally, another three and a third percent for the Welfare Tithe: three required tithes for a total of twenty-three and third percent (23.3%) that the law said a Jew was required to give each year.

So, when my clients asked about the percentage they should give, I would say, "If you want to follow the old tithing system, your answer is for you to give twenty-three and a third percent! And, let's say you are only giving ten percent now. That means you are short thirteen and a third percent this year. How many years have you only been giving ten percent, by the way?"

There is a noticeable dead silence at this point in the conversation. Naturally, the conversation shifts a good bit here, and the individuals want to talk about giving under grace. They rationalize, "It HAS to be better than giving under the law!"

"Okay," I say, "let's talk about grace giving," and I will go back to 2 Corinthians 9:

> Each one must do just as he has purposed **in his heart,** not grudgingly or under compulsion, **for God loves a cheerful giver**.

We are to give from our hearts, and you are to give based on how much you appreciate what the Lord has done for you. You are to give based on how blessed you feel with what the Lord has given you. You are to give based on your heartfelt love for the Lord because the Lord has changed your life. You are to give to the Lord out of love for Him, understanding the truth that He sacrificed Himself for you.

So, how much do you really love the Lord? Do you give based on that love?

This principle is pure and simple: giving is a **pure reflection of your love for the Lord**. There should be no equivocation on this fact. The love of the Lord in your heart will activate you to give to support His Church. If you love Him, you will support His Church. The more love you have for Him, the more you will support His Church. So, I would turn back to my clients and ask, "So, you want to talk about the law again?"

In our heart of hearts, we should reply that all our money is the Lord's. He owns it all. He gives freely to us. My love for the Lord should not only be overflowing in music as I sing the hymn, "I Love You, Lord." The love should show up in what I give each week, month, or year to Him to support the building of His Church. Giving is not just financial because it is a service gift as well. But some of it must be financial, otherwise the Lord would not have shown up at the treasury to watch that old widow with two small coins drop them into the temple box – out of her deep poverty. If her kind of love doesn't light you up, then I do not know what will. Her love for God was exemplary!

Israel was to be solely focused on the love for God at the beginning of each day. As they rose for the day and began to leave their homes, they would recite the *Shema* from Deuteronomy 6. "Hear, O Israel, the Lord is our God, the Lord is One. You shall love the Lord your God with all your..."

All your what?

All your heart!

> "Hear, O Israel! The LORD is our God, the LORD is one! **You shall love the LORD your God with all your heart** and with all your soul and with all your might.
>
> These words, which I am commanding you today, **shall be on your heart**.
>
> **You shall teach them diligently to your sons** and shall talk of them when you sit in your house and when you walk by the way and when you lie down and when you rise up. You shall bind them as a sign on your hand and they shall be as frontals on your forehead. You shall write them on the doorposts of your house and on your gates" (Deuteronomy 6:4-9).

Israel's love for God was to be the primary motivation for everything the people did. They were to teach their children this principle. They were to measure their actions against this principle. They were to place the words on the posts of their doors to be sure to remember them. Their heart motivation was to come first.

What does the heart lead you to do when it comes to supporting His Church?

What is the most memorized verse in the entire Bible? Many would say it is John 3:16:

> **For God so loved the world, <u>that He gave</u>** His only begotten Son, that whoever believes in Him shall not perish, but have eternal life.

When your heart is changed by God, you naturally will love Him. When you understand the truth of the gospel and realize His impact on your life, your love for Him will start and continue to grow. God's example in sending Jesus to us was that He loved us so much that He gave. True love generates a giving spirit. Paul noted the fruit of the Spirit in his letter to the Galatians:

> But the fruit of the Spirit is love, joy, peace, patience, kindness, goodness, faithfulness, gentleness, self-control; against such things there is no law (Galatians 5:22-23).

The first fruit in the list is love, followed by a host of other manifestations of the Spirit's effect on our lives. Your love for Him and your heartfelt appreciation for Him should factor into what you give because if you have a changed heart, it should be reflected in your giving to His Church.

An assessment of the modern church today shows that the charitable giving of our time is down across the board. The U.S. Department of Labor, believe it or not, conducts a survey of individuals about their practices and generates quarterly reports. The department calculates how much time an average worker will spend volunteering at charitable organizations. They actually track and report this information. I really don't know why they do, but it is of great interest to me. What the most recent reports state is that, over the last five years, our time spent in charitable operations is on the decline. Use of our personal time in support of charities is falling precipitously. Perhaps it is more of a "me generation" change, but it is going downhill very quickly. What about financial giving? Financial giving is on a decline as well. Churches are reporting a definitive drop in giving. Attendance at most churches has flatlined or is fading altogether. Commentators maintain that there is an overall spiritual decline all over the world, and that observation may be true. We should be more specific to the motivation, however: over all, the love for God is on the decline. If you love Him, you are part of His flock that continues to support His Church. If you give bountifully, of both your time and your financial resources, and you do so with a pure heartfelt motivation, it is a positive sign that you love God.

Sign #4 – Being Part of His Mission

Our example for everything in life is Jesus. Did Jesus obey God the Father's words? Did Jesus incorporate God's words into His earthly life? Did Jesus recite, value, and teach the Father's words? Did He give?

> Greater love has no one than this, that one lay down his life for his friends (John 15:13).

Jesus turned to His friends and said, "You guys are my friends. I'm going to lay my life down for you." In turn, if we love Him, we will lay down our lives for Him. As we read earlier, Peter boldly stated that he would do that (John 13:37) and, according to historical accounts, DID lay down his life for Jesus. He was crucified upside down because he did not believe he was worthy to be crucified as Jesus was. Eusebius (in A.D. 325) claimed in his *Ecclesiastical History* that all the apostles were martyred except John. The evidence for some of these executions is very spotty, but the number, variety, and quality of testimony to the deaths of both Peter and later Paul in Rome are such that we can presume that both died as martyrs. The early church fathers were unanimous in claiming that Peter died in Rome, by crucifixion, during the persecution of Nero in AD 64. His crucifixion upside down is also recorded, although the evidence is weaker. The apocryphal *Acts of Peter* records the earliest reference to Peter's crucifixion upside down. We can be assured that the Twelve all gave their lives in service to Jesus and His Church. We should be committed to do the same.

Jesus made disciples out of the Twelve as evidenced by each of them giving his life for Him. Jesus was the supreme example of a disciple maker. If you love Him, you accept His mission as your own, so you are committed to make others His disciples.

Jesus called His disciples back to Galilee, and Matthew records:

> Jesus came up and spoke to them, saying, "All authority has been given to Me in heaven and on earth.
>
> **Go therefore and make disciples of all the nations,** *baptizing them in the name of the Father and the Son and the Holy Spirit,* teaching them to observe all that I commanded you; *and lo, I am with you always, even to the end of the age"* (Matthew 28:18-20).

The risen Jesus gave His Church its future mission: to make disciples of all the nations. That mission includes reaching them with the truth of the gospel so that they can be set free (John 8:32). Members of His church should be dedicating considerable portions of their lives to spreading Jesus's story and "being able to make a defense for the hope" that is in them (1 Peter 3:15). If you cannot explain what the gospel is, then it will certainly be tough to defend it.

A commitment to personal evangelism and disciple making seemingly is not common among those Christians who seem to question what making disciples entails in the modern world and what true discipleship is. Bill Hull, an author on the subject of discipleship for more than twenty years, expounded on Matthew 28:18-20, exploring both historical and modern applications of Jesus's Great Commission call to His disciples. In his book, *The Disciple-Making Church*, Hull explained that every disciple should make disciples and that the commitment to disciple making is the calling for every church. Many Christians would agree with that premise, but few seem to understand the extent of the task. When Jesus said, "Go, therefore, and make disciples of all nations," He launched a ministry that continues today in varying forms and successes. Some see His call to Christians as one solely based on evangelism and spreading the Good News to everyone they encounter. Others passionately herald the call as requiring Christians to pursue dedicated discipleship which includes deep theological teaching and application in every phase of a new believer's life.

Some Christians disagree over what Jesus meant in His final message and question if He spoke about evangelism or discipleship and whether the two are the same or if they are separate phases in the Christian life. Christians also tend to disagree over whether evangelism is a spiritual gift given only to certain believers or a natural reaction of all believers to the grace afforded them. Some also are unclear as to whether evangelism simply means preaching the good news or if it includes active and dedicated follow-up.

To the faithful brother Philemon, Paul wrote, "I pray that the sharing of your faith may become effective for the full knowledge of every good thing that is in us for the sake of Christ" (Philemon 1:6). This passage underscores the idea that the sharing of faith has a sanctifying purpose and should lead into a deeper knowledge about the Christ whom Christians proclaim. This deeper knowledge might be considered as the essence of true discipleship, being made into His image over time (2 Corinthians 3:18) because, according to Hull, "evangelism and discipleship (as it is commonly understood)—are really the front side and back side of the same coin. The coin is discipleship."[6] British pastor and veteran discipleship author, Mike

---

[6] Bill Hull and Bobby Harrington, "Why Discipleship Is Better than Evangelism - Discipleship.Org," accessed October 23, 2019, https://discipleship.org/discipleship/why-discipleship-is-better-than-evangelism/#.XbCe5lVKipo.

Breen, maintained that "more often than not, leaders claim that we have an evangelism problem in the Church today with declining attendance, baptisms and other significant metrics. [However], we don't have an evangelism problem; we have a discipleship problem."[7]

Is there really a difference between evangelism and making disciples?

In 2016 the Barna Group conducted a "State of the Church" survey on the religious practices of approximately 5,000 Americans. The results indicated that fifty-five percent of the respondents had been to a church service within the past six months.[8] The remaining forty-five percent, referred to as the "unchurched," had not been in a church service within the last six months. The Barna Group noted that the latter group of individuals could have been "de-churched," meaning they had a prior relationship with a church but had given up

---

[7] Mike Breen, *Building a Discipling Culture: How to Release a Missional Movement by Discipling People Like Jesus Did* (Pawley's Island, SC: 3DM Publishing, 2011), 5.

[8] Barna Group, "The State of the Church 2016 - Barna Group," https://www.barna.com/research/state-church-2016/.

on the faith or the local body to which they had previously belonged. Of the churched respondents, forty-six percent generally believed that "Christians have a responsibility to evangelize others." However, results of the survey also revealed that a mere <u>seven percent</u> of these respondents practice their faith in such a way as to identify themselves as evangelical Christians. The survey definition included the sharing of faith in Christ with others as a defining characteristic of "evangelical."[9]

Discipleship should be multifaceted and holistic, as well as all-encompassing and transformative over time. Discipleship should involve taking the initiative to acquire biblical knowledge, as well as utilizing that knowledge in service to others. Without both components true discipleship does not occur. Jesus called us to make disciples of all the nations. We can only succeed by setting an example for them over time, so WE need to be disciples ourselves. If only seven percent of those individuals who identify as evangelical

---

[9] Ibid. These conditions include saying their faith is very important in their life today; believing they have a personal responsibility to share their religious beliefs about Christ with non-Christians and do so; believing that Satan exists; believing that Jesus Christ lived a sinless life on earth; asserting that the Bible is accurate in all that it teaches; believing that eternal salvation is possible only through grace, not works; and describing God as the all-knowing, all-powerful, perfect deity who created the universe and still rules it today.

Christians are actively involved in sharing their faith and making disciples, it is no wonder the church is seeing a decline in attendance and financial support.

The mandate is clear from the final directions from the Lord in Matthew 28:18-20. The Lord first spoke of this labor of love to His disciples, telling them that "the harvest is plentiful, but the workers are few. Therefore, beseech the Lord of the harvest to send out workers into His harvest" (Matthew 9:37-38). Christians are not to hoard the glorious message of grace but are to go out into the harvest, always being ready to make a defense (1 Peter 3:15). Bobby Harrington, lead pastor of Harpeth Christian Church in Franklin, Tennessee, and Hull collaborated to author two books on discipleship which became the genus of the discipleship.org website. Harrington described his experiences with early evangelistic efforts as short-sighted and wrote that the greatest lesson he learned from those experiences is that evangelism and discipleship must be aligned.[10] Harrington explained that having one without the other fails to fulfill the calling to follow Jesus and noted:

---

[10] Bill Hull and Bobby Harrington, "Why Discipleship is Better than Evangelism - Discipleship.Org," https://discipleship.org/discipleship/why-discipleship-is-better-than-evangelism/#.XbCe5lVKipo.

Discipleship without evangelism creates the very
unhealthy condition of sterility in followers of Christ.
Christians who do not evangelize are not fulfilled in their
lives, and they take on a certain intramural pettiness.
When people are educated beyond their level of
obedience, they become religious schizophrenics, experts
on what they are not experiencing.[11]

While acquisition of knowledge is important, the dispensing of

knowledge must also be present to have a fulfilled life in Christ and

to fulfill His mission. If you love Him, you will work diligently to

support His mission.

Think about the first time you fell in love with someone. Perhaps the

individual you loved became your spouse. Perhaps the individual is

no longer a part of your life. Regardless of the current situation,

remember how you were when this relationship was in its infancy.

How often did you speak about this individual to others, perhaps to

close friends or to your immediate family? With great joy you loved

to speak about this individual as you felt that emotional love surge

through you. I can still remember that moment in my life. Think

about the time you bought your first new car. That new car smell

wafted over as you got into the car. You loved to show off that car to

---

[11] Ibid.

others, to take them for rides in it, to speak about all the various features of the car.

Was there a time in your life where you spoke about Jesus the same way? If you have trusted Jesus with your life, can you remember when that process began? Did you long to tell anyone about Him? Were you excited to have the opportunity to explain the change in your life to anyone who would listen?

Do you have the same desire today? Is that love relationship with Jesus still so vibrant that you love to discuss Him, love to share the story of when you trusted Him, and tell how your life has been changed by Him – even today – long after the day when you first were introduced? If not, why is that? Has your love for Him grown so cold that He is no longer shared like the once new car that is now just "my old car"?

While there are many ways to share Jesus with others, the goal of this book does not include an explanation of the ways this sharing can happen. Personally, I believe that learning as many ways as possible will aide you in being prepared to make a defense of your belief in Him. There is no one "right way" to share your faith. I learned the *Romans Road* early in my walk with Christ. I learned how to lead someone through the *Four Spiritual Laws* in order to go into prison ministry. I learned to share Christ using *The Hand* as a part of Evangelism Explosion. I learned how to share Jesus using *The Wordless Book*, Spurgeon's easy method for instructing children about the gospel and Jesus's sacrifice for us. I also learned how to use a basketball court, a hurdle on a running track, a long jump, a high jump, the trees and flowers outside my house, and the lines on a sidewalk. All of these different ways, the knowledge gained, and the plans of salvation memorized mean nothing unless they are engaged into action because of your love for Jesus.

I love to develop ways to engage in conversation with others about Jesus. Our community group at church was studying the End Times, and I was reminded that Revelation 12 was an excellent path to sharing our faith in Christ. We created a sample tract, a detailed conversation between a believer and a non-believer about the events of the world that are described in Revelation 12. The construction of that conversational tract involved a large group of individuals who made the document much better than the draft I had composed all those years before. The group adopted it as a mission to share it with others, to send it out to loved ones and acquaintances who do not know Jesus as Savior and Lord. You can find that conversational tract in Appendix A for your reading and edification.

Making disciples starts with evangelism and telling how the story of Jesus affects your life. R. C. Sproul explained that he had much difficulty in his early Christian experience with the Great Commission. He believed he was not particularly good at evangelism and regarded himself close to a failure.[12] Eventually he learned that "we should take notice of what Jesus did not say in the Great Commission. He did not say, 'Go therefore and make converts of as many people as possible.'" Discipleship, then, became the focus of Sproul's ministry, Ligonier Ministries:

> The Great Commission is the call of Christ for His disciples to extend His authority over the whole world. We are to share the gospel with everyone so that more and more people might call Him "Master." This calling is not simply a call to evangelism. It isn't merely a call to get students for our seminaries, our colleges, or for Ligonier Ministries. Rather, Christ calls us to make disciples. Disciples are people who have committed in their hearts and minds to follow the thinking and conduct of the Master forever. Such discipleship is a lifelong experience.[13]

---

[12] R. C. Sproul, "We're Called to Make Disciples, Not Simply Converts," https://www.ligonier.org/blog/were-called-make-disciples-not-simply-converts/.

[13] Ibid.

Sproul's ministry and discipleship focus took him across the globe where he shared the gospel with many. He aggressively pursued those who came to Christ with a concentrated effort of education about what a disciple should be. His perceived early failures were trumped by a consistent passion to call believers to commit to the Master.

I believe success in evangelism is simple. Our job is not to make converts to Christianity. In fact, I believe it is impossible for us to "make a convert." For anyone to come to Jesus Christ in saving faith, the Holy Spirit has to work in his or her life. Usually this work has begun long before we would engage in conversation with this individual and the conversation is a team effort. As Paul wrote to Corinthians, "I planted, Apollos watered, but God was causing the growth. So then neither the one who plants nor the one who waters is anything, but God who causes the growth" (1 Corinthians 3:6-7). This is true of the initial coming to faith in Jesus as well as the continual growth after one comes to Christ. Without God choosing the individual before the creation of the Earth, Paul writes, salvation of one will never happen (Ephesians 1:4-5). Our job is to continue to spread the gospel message. If we want success in evangelism, we need to follow a couple simple tasks and we are guaranteed to have success.

Joshua was given a formula for success by God early in his life and was called by God to take over for Moses after he died on the precipice of the Promised Land. God said:

> Just as I have been with Moses, I will be with you; I will not fail you or forsake you. **Be strong and courageous**, for you shall give this people possession of the land which I swore to their fathers to give them. **Only be strong and very courageous;** be careful to do according to all the law which Moses My servant commanded you; do not turn from it to the right or to the left, so **that you may have success wherever you go**.
>
> **This book of the law shall not depart from your mouth, but you shall meditate on it day and night, so that you may be careful to do according to all that is written in it; for then you will make your way prosperous, and then you will have success.**
>
> **Have I not commanded you? Be strong and courageous!** Do not tremble or be dismayed, for the LORD your God is with you wherever you go (Joshua 1:5-8).

God wanted to make sure that Joshua knew that God was the one in control of the events that Joshua would face.

Joshua had two tasks.

First, he was supposed to be strong and courageous. Whatever events that would occur as he led the people, Joshua was supposed to trust in God's provision and protection. God said that He would not fail or forsake Joshua and that He would be with him just as God had been with Moses. God told Joshua three times that he needed to be strong and courageous, so this command must have been important! God knew that the tasks in front of Joshua might make him fearful or wary of stepping out in faith. If Joshua were strong and courageous, however, he would have success because he would be trusting God, not himself.

Second, Joshua was supposed to dedicate himself to following the book of the law and committed to mediating on the law. Joshua was to live a life committed to the principles God had described. If Joshua meditated on the Word, he would have "head knowledge" of these principles. We would say that he was book smart, knowing what the Word contained and how to describe its contents to others. Joshua's knowledge of the Word had to be greater than just head knowledge, however. He was called by God to "be careful to do according to all that is written in it," meaning, Joshua was to have experiential knowledge of the Word. He was to live out what he had learned by studying the Word. In short, he was to become a disciple! If Joshua became a disciple, he was guaranteed to have success.

Paul told Timothy to be bold and courageous, writing in his last letter that "God gave us a spirit not of fear but of power and love and self-control" (2 Timothy 1:7). Jesus said, "If anyone comes to Me, and does not hate his own father and mother and wife and children and brothers and sisters, yes, and even his own life, he cannot be My disciple. Whoever does not carry his own cross and come after Me cannot be My disciple" (Luke 14:26-27). He continued, "So then, none of you can be My disciple who does not give up all his own possessions. Therefore, salt is good; but if even salt has become tasteless, with what will it be seasoned? It is useless either for the soil or for the manure pile; it is thrown out. He who has ears to hear, let him hear" (Luke 14:33-35). The priority of Jesus' message was that His teaching must become the predominant influence on a disciple's life and that a life of discipleship includes prioritizing His call over worldly distractions and possessions. Christians are not to be fearful because that spirit of fear does not come from God. On the other hand, we are to commit ourselves to discipleship as the priority of our lives.

We recently surveyed our church membership about their evangelism practices. Knowing the findings from Barna survey of 2016, our leadership wanted to know if our congregation was better than the average. The personal evangelism and disciple making survey questions included questions about heart commitment as well as practical commitment. Heart commitment questions addressed the desire of the survey participants to be disciple makers, whereas practical commitment questions focused on the respondents' past, current, and planned evangelistic or disciple making activities. A belief that sharing faith in Jesus is critical to disciple making was clear from looking at the survey responses.

Most members had hearts committed to evangelism. The practical commitment questions, on the other hand, showed a reluctance to be active in the sharing of faith. Specifically, the survey asked for primary and secondary obstacles to sharing faith in Jesus.

Not surprisingly, fear of rejection was high along with not having opportunity:

Obstacles to Sharing My Faith	Primary	Secondary	%
Lack of Opportunity	11	9	22%
Fear of Rejection	11	5	18%
Missing Opportunities	6	6	13%
Feel Like I'm Selling Something	1	8	10%
Not My Gift	4	5	10%
Lack of Knowledge	2	5	8%
Lack of Time	1	2	3%

If you view success as simply sharing the message of Jesus, however, your perspective should be different. Your sole job as a believer is to communicate the gospel to others and, regardless of how others respond, you will be considered faithful to God if you are committed to the task. Should you know what to say? Of course. If your life is dedicated to the Word and meditating on it, I guarantee you will have something to say when the conversation begins. How am I so confident in this fact? Jesus gave us the promise that it would happen:

> The Helper, the Holy Spirit, whom the Father will send in My name, He will teach you all things, and **bring to your remembrance** all that I said to you (John 14:26).

The Holy Spirit who indwells you will give you the words. Isn't that an amazing thought? If you are lost for words, fear not, Christian. The Holy Spirit will provide remembrance when you need it.

Jesus continued, saying:

> When He [The Holy Spirit] comes, **will convict the world concerning sin and righteousness and judgment**; concerning sin, because they do not believe in Me; and concerning righteousness, because I go to the Father and you no longer see Me; and concerning judgment, because the ruler of this world has been judged. I have many more things to say to you, but you cannot bear [them] now. **But when He, the Spirit of truth, comes, He will guide you into all the truth**; for He will not speak on His own

initiative, but whatever He hears, He will speak; and He
will disclose to you what is to come (John 16:8-13).

The role of the Holy Spirit IS to convict the peoples of the world
about their individual sin, about the righteousness of God, and about
the coming judgment of Jesus. It is the **Holy Spirit's job** to make
converts, not ours. It is also the Holy Spirit's role "to guide you into
all truth." While it is an excellent task to commit yourself to
memorizing Bible verses, some Christians do not have the ability to
retain this knowledge. As we age, retaining the exact words of the
Bible fade from easy recall. Trust me! Isn't it nice to know that,
should forgetfulness occur, the Holy Spirit, who knows all truth, will
guide you into all truth when you need recall? I cannot tell you how
many times verses I had read and memorized years ago come
flooding back to my mind just when I need them. Whatever words
might come out of my mouth, I know that the Holy Spirit will take
them and use them as He chooses.

What happens if they do not respond? Jesus said,

If anyone will not receive you or listen to your words,
shake off the dust from your feet when you leave that
house or town. Truly, I say to you, it will be more bearable
on the day of judgment for the land of Sodom and
Gomorrah than for that town" (Matthew 10:14).

Jesus did not say the disciples would be a failure if people did not respond positively to their message. On the contrary, Jesus told them to continue their communication of the message in another location. Immediately before sending them out, Jesus said, "The harvest is plentiful, but the laborers are few; therefore, pray earnestly to the Lord of the harvest to send out laborers into his harvest" (Matthew 9:37-38). Jesus was preparing them to go forth and harvest His crop: the Church. The disciples were the laborers, and so are we to be laborers in our generation.

Christians are to boldly go and tell the story of Jesus to others, and we will be successful because of our obedience in going out into the harvest and communicating the gospel message to anyone we can. The results of those encounters belong to God. Many ways exist to share His message and be part of His mission. When you love someone, you love to talk about that individual. If you find yourself talking about Jesus to others, it is a positive sign that you love Him and love supporting His mission. If you are not part of His mission, however, you should be concerned. If you love Him, you should want others to love Him as you do.

Sign #5 – The Feeding of His Sheep

After Jesus died for us on the cross, He was resurrected by God the Father and again walked the Earth among the disciples. There are many recorded sightings of the resurrected Jesus in the Bible. Paul lists seven specific times Jesus appeared (1 Corinthians 15:5-8). Sometimes He allowed Himself to be identified quickly (John 20, e.g.), but other times He did not (Luke 24, e.g.). As you can imagine, the disciples were in a bit of confusion after the crucifixion. Their entire belief system of Jesus's reigning on Earth was immediately thrown into chaos, and they were suddenly on their own. In one of His early appearances after the Resurrection, Jesus told His female disciples to inform the Twelve that they should meet Him in Galilee (Matthew 28:7-10). In John 21 the Apostle records a scene where some of Jesus's disciples are in Galilee waiting for the Lord to appear. The walk to Galilee from Jerusalem gave them time to think about the crucifixion and the empty tomb. Peter, no doubt, was thinking about how he denied the Lord three times as Jesus had predicted (Luke 22:54-62). After a long time waiting in Galilee for the Lord to appear, Peter made a decision because he was tired of waiting:

> Simon Peter, Thomas (called the Twin), Nathanael of Cana in Galilee, the sons of Zebedee, and two others of his

disciples were together. Simon Peter said to them, **"I am going fishing."**

They said to him, "We will go with you." They went out and got into the boat, but that night they caught nothing (John 21:2-3).

Peter decided to go fishing. This choice should have been no surprise because Peter was trained as a fisherman. He and his brother Andrew were fishermen as were James and John, the sons of Zebedee. Yet, there was a finality to Peter's declaration. He had given the Lord three years of his life. He gave his commitment to the Lord because he thought the Lord was establishing His kingdom on the Earth, and he wanted to be a part of that plan. That plan obviously did not come to fulfillment, however, and Peter determined to go back to his old profession. He was going <u>back</u> to fishing. Peter, as the oldest of the Twelve, usually set the tone for the group. He often voiced the intents and feelings of the others. In this case, his decision to go fishing caused the others to join him. At least four of disciples, and perhaps all six in this scene, were going with him. Their defection did not result in any immediate success, however, as they caught no fish after working all night. Jesus appears the next morning, but the disciples did not know that it was He. Jesus announces that there is an abundance of fish next to the boats, the Apostle John recognizes that it is the Lord, and Peter jumps into the water to get to Jesus as fast as he can. When the remaining disciples make it to shore with all the fish, Jesus is ready with charcoals and prepares breakfast for the group. After breakfast, Jesus has the disciples' complete attention. He looked at Peter and said, "Simon, son of John, do you love me more than these?" Jesus does not call him "Peter," as He did before many times (Matthew 16:18, e.g.). Instead, Jesus uses Peter's old name, "Simon." Commentators often mention that Jesus used Peter's old name because Peter was acting like his old self. Jesus asked Peter if he loved Him "more than these." The term "these" could have meant the fish to whom Peter had decided to return, but most likely Jesus was referring to the other disciples. Peter's response was clear, "Yes, Lord; you know that I love you."

The Greek language has four widely used words for "love." *Eros* is a passionate love, most often used to describe an erotic or sexual love; *Storge* is a familial love or an instant, natural affection; *Phileo* is a brotherly, sisterly or friendly love; and *Agape* is the highest, most noble, sacrificial love. When Jesus asks Peter if he loves Him, Jesus uses a form of *Agape*. When Peter responds, he uses a form of *Phileo*. It is as if Jesus asked Peter, "Do you love Me?" and Peter replied, "I like you a lot, Lord." Peter had previously committed that he would go to death for the Lord even if all the other disciples failed

Him (Matthew 26:35) only to have gone back on his commitment and denied Jesus. He was in no frame of mind to purport that his love for Jesus was sacrificial enough to use the word form of *Agape*. Jesus then tells Peter, "Feed My lambs." The Greek word for "lambs," *arnion*, is used to describe younger sheep.[14] The Greek word for "feed," *bosko*, means to nourish by feeding. Jesus's command to Peter is that he needed to commit to giving continual spiritual nourishment to the Lord's people, which included the other disciples with them that day. Instead of leading them into defection, Peter was called to lead them into spiritual growth.

Jesus asked Peter, a second time, "Simon, son of John, do you love me?" He said to him, "Yes, Lord; you know that I love you." Both Jesus and Peter used the same Greek words as they did in the first exchange. This time, however, Jesus told Peter, "Shepherd my sheep." The Greek word for "shepherd," *poimano*, means "to guard, care for, and protect."[15] The Greek word "sheep," *probation*, is used

---

[14] Wesley J. Perschbacher, ed., *The New Analytical Greek Lexicon* (Peabody, MA: Hendrickson, 1990), *arnion*, 53.

[15] Ibid., *poimano*, 331.

for older sheep.[16] Jesus was calling Peter to a lifetime of caring for and protecting the Lord's people.

Jesus asked Peter a third time, "Simon, son of John, do you love me?" John records that Peter was grieved that the Lord asked him again. The difference in this exchange was that Jesus did not use a form of *Agape* but instead used a form of *Phileo*. In other words, Jesus was asking Peter, "Do you even like Me as a brother?" No wonder Peter was grieved. Jesus was questioning if Peter could be trusted. Peter said to him, "Lord, you know everything; you know that I love you," again using *Phileo* as he had earlier. Peter's past actions could not confirm that he was trustworthy. He had failed the Lord and was at the peak of embarrassment. The only hope Peter had was that the Lord knew what he was feeling at that moment: his desperation to be faithful to the very end. Jesus said to him, "Feed my sheep. The Greek word for "feed" is that same word, *bosko.* Jesus was calling Peter to provide spiritual nourishment to both the younger and older group of the Lord's people.

This exchange between Jesus and Peter provides us the next positive sign: if you love God, you will feed and care for His people.

---

[16] Ibid., *probation*, 344.

The natural question concerning this passage in John 21 is "Doesn't this passage apply to Pastors and Elders?" Most certainly the answer is YES. The resurrected Jesus was mentoring the men who would continue His teaching ministry on earth. Jesus was prophesied to fill this role for His men with the prophet Isaiah's noting that "He will tend His flock like a shepherd; He will gather the lambs in His arms; He will carry them in His bosom, and gently lead those who are young" (Isaiah 40:11). Jesus's life was that of the example Shepherd, working to restore Peter after his failures, caring for those young men, and providing firm guidance when needed.

Peter certainly regarded himself as an Elder when he wrote:

> Therefore, **I exhort the elders among you, as your fellow elder** and witness of the sufferings of Christ, and a partaker also of the glory that is to be revealed, **shepherd the flock of God among you**, exercising oversight not under compulsion, but **voluntarily**, according to the will of God; and not for sordid gain, but with eagerness; nor yet as lording it over those allotted to your charge, but **proving to be examples to the flock** (1 Peter 5:1-3).

Nearing the end of his ministry, Peter sought to instruct the next generation about the principles that Jesus gave him. No doubt, the interaction with Jesus (as John recorded in John 21) was impactful on his life and ministry. Going from the abandonment of the Lord's plan

116

for his life and returning to being solely a fisherman to renewing his life commitment to Jesus and His commandments set the Apostle up for great influence. Initially, Peter focused on teaching his Jewish friends and countrymen. Then Peter was given a vision of a Gentile named Cornelius calling to him from Caesarea (Acts 10), and he began to feed men from every nation. At the end of his life, those same words that Jesus gave him as instruction Peter was passing on to other elders, calling them to "shepherd the flock of God," not only to do the work but to prove "to be examples to the flock." No doubt, some of those in Peter's initial audience for his letter were pastors and teachers whom he commanded to feed the sheep as well. It is the multi-generational call for a pastor or elder to continue to teach and hold other men accountable to Jesus's commandments.

Paul, nearing the end of his personal ministry, wrote similar instructions to Timothy, calling him to remember "the things which you have heard from me in the presence of many witnesses" and then to "entrust these to faithful men who will be able to teach others also" (2 Timothy 2:2). Four generations of disciples are shown in this verse: Paul, Timothy, those Timothy would instruct to be elders, and the faithful disciples that those elders would teach.

James wrote that pastors and elders (and all Bible teachers) will receive a stricter judgment (James 3:1) because these men are feeding Jesus's sheep. Paul wrote to Titus telling him to "speak the things which are fitting for sound doctrine." Paul also instructed Timothy with this judgment in mind writing:

> **If anyone advocates a different doctrine and does not agree with sound words**, those of our Lord Jesus Christ, and with the doctrine conforming to godliness, **he is conceited and understands nothing**; but he has a morbid interest in controversial questions and disputes about words, out of which arise envy, strife, abusive language, evil suspicions, and constant friction between men of depraved mind and deprived of the truth, who suppose that godliness is a means of gain (1 Timothy 6:3-5).

Paul's expectation was that Timothy would continue in the same teaching and would faithfully carry out the ministry of boldly instructing others. Paul notes that many men will not be faithful in this ministry. These men will have different motives in mind, or they will not be diligent to ensure that what they say matches the teaching that Paul learned from Jesus and communicated to others in his lifetime of ministry. Feeding Jesus's sheep means that the pastor or elder needs to ensure that they have the correct recipe.

Paul's expectation was a serious one, making it an oath to remain faithful, writing to Timothy:

I solemnly charge you in the presence of God and of Christ Jesus, who is to judge the living and the dead, and by His appearing and His kingdom: **preach the word; be ready in season and out of season; reprove, rebuke, exhort, with great patience and instruction.** For the time will come when they will not endure sound doctrine; but wanting to have their ears tickled, they will accumulate for themselves teachers in accordance to their own desires, and will turn away their ears from the truth and will turn aside to myths (2 Timothy 4:3-4).

In other words, Paul says, "Timothy, feed Jesus's sheep; do it when they want to hear it, and even when they do not want to hear it." Because, Paul writes, many of them will accumulate their own teachers that they wish to hear and stray away from the truth. Timothy was to continue feeding with great patience and instruction. Caring and feeding for sheep takes patience, and pastors need to learn that this level of care is paramount to the success of Jesus's mission.

So, if you are not a pastor or elder, does that mean Jesus's call in John 21 should mean nothing to you? NO. All of us are required to feed our sheep! I guarantee that there is someone you know who knows less about Jesus than you do.

If you are a father or mother or a grandfather or grandmother, then you also have a flock to feed among you. You need to be the primary shepherd of that flock of God. Your pastor or elder cannot, as much as they may try, have the effect on your children that you will. Your children need to see the gospel lived out in front of them every day. If the gospel teaching is real to you, it will be real to those children. On the other hand, if your children do not see the gospel lived out in front of them, they will not perceive it as very important for them. Children observe everything in their environment. They will certainly remember (and sometimes point out) where you have missed or forgotten an important gospel element.

I remember a time after church when our children were quite young. A few families from our church went out to lunch together, and we were enjoying conversing about the day and the specifics of that day's sermon. So engrossed were we in our conversation that the food came, and everyone started eating. Five minutes into the meal, my five-year old daughter announced to the group (quite loudly), "WE FORGOT THE BLESSING!" Well, there was no mistake about that missed gospel element: everyone immediately stopped, and the blessing of prayer ensued.

Children must be fed, and parents must do the feeding. From an early age, your children should be immersed in the Bible and its life-altering words. There is never an inappropriate time to share the gospel in song, in poems, in family Bible reading moments, or in general conversations about your life with Jesus. I smile as I think of the effect my bride has had on our granddaughter. This beautiful young lady, all of two years old, sings "Jesus Loves Me" while she plays on a playground or roams around the house playing with her toys. Her singing is communal, a seemingly mindless repetition of the teaching that she has received. She knows the truth: Jesus loves her. May we all feed our little lambs in this way!

It is important not only to tell of all those wonderful moments with Jesus but to also share your life failures. The gospel becomes real to your children when they realize that YOU are not perfect, just forgiven. They will understand that THEY do not have to be perfect, just forgiven. This is one of the mistakes I made as a young parent. When the inevitable moments of failure happened in my life, I dealt with it privately. I missed one of the greatest opportunities to explain the gospel to our kids. Do not make my mistake! Treat moments of failure as the best sermon material you could ever find.

Paul had this attitude in his life. One can hear his anguish when he wrote Romans 7:14-24:

> For we know that the Law is spiritual, but I am of flesh,
> sold into bondage to sin. For what I am doing, I do not

understand; for **I am not practicing what I would like to do**, but **I am doing the very thing I hate**. But if I do the very thing I do not want to do, I agree with the Law, confessing that the Law is good. So now, no longer am I the one doing it, but sin which dwells in me. For I know that nothing good dwells in me, that is, in my flesh; for the willing is present in me, but the doing of the good is not. **For the good that I want, I do not do, but I practice the very evil that I do not want.** But if I am doing the very thing I do not want, I am no longer the one doing it, but sin which dwells in me.

I find then the principle that evil is present in me, the one who wants to do good. For I joyfully concur with the law of God in the inner man, but I see a different law in the members of my body, waging war against the law of my mind and making me a prisoner of the law of sin which is in my members.

Wretched man that I am! Who will set me free from the body of this death?

Paul is wrestling with his emotional impulses and the decisions of his life. Some commentators maintain that Paul is speaking of moments of his life prior to coming to Christ in order to perpetuate the thought that the Christian life is free from struggle. Hogwash! The teaching that Christian life is free from struggle is not sound doctrine. Paul is writing about his experience after coming to Christ and even considering the impulses and decisions that are affecting him when he writes these words. Paul calls himself "wretched" and in desperate need of being freed from his condition. The Greek word "wretched" means to be beaten-down from continued strain, leaving a person literally full of callouses and deep misery – describing a person with severe side-effects from great, ongoing strain. Paul would not have felt this deep misery before he came to Christ; he would have been oblivious to it. It is only after coming to know the truth, knowing what the law was intended to do, and realizing that one is in dire need of rescue from the law that Paul writes these words. Paul uses the word for callous which we use to describe the hardening of the skin that forms over an injury and pictures healing followed by more injury and then further healing. Paul is in agony over his condition. He has been continually broken and repaired, again and again, through his life. Sharing his mistakes with his sheep gives them the confidence to deal with their own struggles and failures in life.

But Paul does not leave himself without hope as the next verse shows from whom his hope comes: **Thanks be to God through Jesus Christ our Lord!** (Romans 7:25)

Paul reassures his audience that Jesus's sacrifice for his personal sins, God's giving of the Holy Spirit as a seal to all believers, and His eternal promise of future redemption <u>will</u> bring about a day when he, as well as all Christians, will have permanent relief from these struggles. In short, the gospel message is the answer. The entire chapter, Romans 8, is a testimony that victory in Jesus Christ is the solution to Paul's problem, and the chapter culminates in that marvelous statement:

> For I am convinced that neither death, nor life, nor angels, nor principalities, nor things present, nor things to come, nor powers, nor height, nor depth, nor any other created thing, will be able to separate us from the love of God, which is in Christ Jesus our Lord (Romans 8:38-39).

Regardless of our struggles in life, if we love God, nothing will be able to separate us from His love for us. This tremendous reassurance IS the gospel message, and we need our children to hear it. We need to feed our sheep the truth and teach that sound doctrine that will give them the same life that it gives us.

Parents are not the only lay people with sheep. If you lead a children's Sunday School class or you lead a Bible study, you should have the same passion for feeding your sheep. It does not matter if people in your class are older than you are. If God has placed you in position of leadership over a group of people, consider them your sheep to feed. If you cannot think of someone in your life that you are currently feeding, find someone to feed. I guarantee you that you probably have greater knowledge and experience than someone you know. We are to help each other in this life on earth.

The care and feeding of sheep has another important component: Jesus's children are all colors, shapes, and sizes. I cannot help but remember the children's song "Jesus Loves the Little Children" with its lyrics, "Red and yellow, black and white; they are precious in His sight; Jesus loves the little children of the world." You may have learned that song as a child as a parent sang it to you or learned it as an adult and have sung it to your children. It is a great reminder that Jesus's focus is greater than we sometimes realize.

At the end of Matthew 25, Jesus shares a promise for the future about God's judgment of the world. Jesus said:

> But when the Son of Man comes in His glory, and all the angels with Him, then He will sit on His glorious throne. All the nations will be gathered before Him; and He will separate them from one another, as the shepherd separates the sheep from the goats; and He will put the sheep on His right, and the goats on the left.

> Then the King will say to those on His right, 'Come, you who are blessed of My Father, inherit the kingdom prepared for you from the foundation of the world. **For I was hungry, and you gave Me something to eat; I was thirsty, and you gave Me something to drink; I was a stranger, and you invited Me in; naked, and you clothed Me; I was sick, and you visited Me; I was in prison, and you came to Me.'**

God, the King, will separate the sheep from the goats. His sheep will have a kingdom prepared for them. One of the signifying characteristics of those who enter the kingdom will be that they have served God: given Him food, drink, clothing, and cared for Him when He was a stranger, when He was in poor health, and when they visited Him when He was in prison.

What? When did these have an opportunity to minister to God?

> Then the righteous will answer Him, 'Lord, when did we see You hungry, and feed You, or thirsty, and give You something to drink? And when did we see You a stranger, and invite You in, or naked, and clothe You? When did we see You sick, or in prison, and come to You?' (Matthew 25:37-39)

They asked that very question of the King, and the King responded:

> 'Truly I say to you, **to the extent that you did it to one of these brothers of Mine, even the least of them, you did it to Me.**'

The general principle is that when you extend care to your brothers and sisters, you are showing your love for God through your actions.

On the other hand, the reverse is true for those who do not extend this love:

126

Then He will also say to those on His left, 'Depart from Me, accursed ones, into the eternal fire which has been prepared for the devil and his angels; for I was hungry, and you gave Me nothing to eat; I was thirsty, and you gave Me nothing to drink; I was a stranger, and you did not invite Me in; naked, and you did not clothe Me; sick, and in prison, and you did not visit Me.'

Then they themselves also will answer, 'Lord, when did we see You hungry, or thirsty, or a stranger, or naked, or sick, or in prison, and did not take care of You?' "Then He will answer them, 'Truly I say to you, to the extent that you did not do it to one of the least of these, you did not do it to Me.'

These will go away into eternal punishment, but the righteous into eternal life.

Jesus's words are not a social gospel message. There is no way to earn yourself a trip to Heaven from a life of good works. In fact, thinking you CAN get there through good works or believing that you are a "good person" is reflective of you NOT being saved. When you are saved, you realize that maintaining these beliefs about salvation is an error. You only get there through grace (Ephesians 2:8-10). However, Jesus teaches that those who ARE His children care for and feed His sheep. His children live a life of service to others and extend love in His name.

The Apostle John lived a life of service like Jesus did. At the end of his life, he wrote:

> And by this we know that we have come to know Him, if we keep his commandments. **Whoever says "I know him" but does not keep His commandments is a liar, and the truth is not in him,** but whoever keeps His word, in him truly the love of God is perfected. **By this we know that we are in Him:** the one who says he abides in Him ought himself to walk in the same manner as He walked (1 John 2:3-6).

How should Jesus's life affect your life? Jesus fed the five thousand. Jesus visited the sick. Jesus wept with those who were weeping. Jesus washed the feet of the Twelve – including Judas (John 13). Jesus served, taught, ministered to many – even those who were not to be in His kingdom. His passion was to follow the Father's will, and the Old Testament is replete with examples of how His people, the Jews, were to care for those around them as a primary extension of God's love for them. Should Christians do otherwise?

If a member of your church is experiencing difficulties, then be the hands of Jesus and give aide. Take a meal to those who need one. Provide clothing to those who have little. Share what God has financially blessed you with and donate to causes that promote His teaching and example. There are a multitude of opportunities around the world to care for others in His name. Trust that He knows what your needs are and that all your needs will be met by Him when you extend yourself in assisting others. Jesus said, "By this all men will know that you are My disciples, if you have love for one another" (John 13:34-35).

Extend His love to those who you might believe, at the present time, are outside the fellowship of His sheep. God's plan for those individuals might be that they are loved into the kingdom. We simply do not know everyone whom God has chosen to be in His kingdom. What we do know is that Jesus gave us the future vision of the judgment, and His people will extend His love to individuals who they do not perceive are part of His kingdom. So, if you love Him, you will extend His love to others regardless of their identification.

Your Personal Evaluation

How did you do? You have read about the reassuring signs that signify that you truly love God.

- If you love Him, you obey His Commandments.
- If you love Him, you study His Word.
- If you love Him, you give in support of His Church.
- If you love Him, you become part of His Mission.
- If you love Him, you will feed His Sheep.

The Apostle Paul wrote:

> Test yourselves to see if you are in the faith; examine yourselves! Or do you not recognize this about yourself; that Jesus Christ is in you – unless you indeed fail the test (2 Corinthians 13:5).

The Bible calls us to self-evaluation. Christians should look at this evaluation as an opportunity to honestly test ourselves and our commitment level. The evaluation should be objective and thorough. Think about a normal day in your life as you wake, as you plan your day, as you work either at home or at an office, and as you relate to others along the way. How much time does God get from you in a normal day? How important is He in your life? How are the gifts that He has given you used?

On a scale of 0 to 5 for each aspect of our walk with Jesus (with 0 being the lowest and 5 being the highest commitment), take a moment to complete an honest assessment of your life right now. No one else is going to know your answers, but this is a moment to ask the Lord, "How deep is my love for God?" He already knows where you are.

How would you evaluate yourself?

Obey His Commandments	0	1	2	3	4	5
Study His Word	0	1	2	3	4	5
Give to His Church	0	1	2	3	4	5
Part of His Mission	0	1	2	3	4	5
Feed His Sheep	0	1	2	3	4	5

Total Score: _____

A score greater than 20 is a solid reassurance of your love for God. You may have areas where you can improve as we all do, but we can be assured we are on the right path in our walk with Jesus.

If your total number is between 10 and 20, then you may have some disciplined work to do in your life. In which area did you give yourself the lowest score? Seek out a spiritual mentor to aide you in growing in that area and pray to God for guidance and a deeper commitment.

A score from 5 to 10 should be concerning to you. Perhaps you should speak with someone you trust about your current relationship with God. Seek a pastor or elder in your church for a conversation about your life in Christ.

If you score is below 5 then 1) either you are a new Christian or 2) there is good chance that Christ does not live inside you. If you are not a new Christian, then seek a pastor or elder to explain salvation to you afresh and anew.

A Warning of the Coming Judgment

The Lord had something to say about the end times in Matthew 7:21-23:

> Not everyone who says to Me, '**Lord, Lord**,' will enter the kingdom of heaven, but he who does the will of
> My Father who is in heaven.

He says "not everyone" who will call "Lord, Lord" will enter the kingdom of heaven. "Not everyone" should be very clear and thought provoking. That is an immediate refutation of universalism, a belief system which maintains that everyone is going to heaven.

When you see "Lord, Lord" in the Bible, or when you see another name repeated as the Lord said to Peter, "Simon, Simon," this use of repeated names is symbolic of intimacy or someone's plea for intimacy. The Lord is telling Peter they have a close relationship, because "I am using the familiar to address you, Peter." Specifically, this pattern is a Hebrew expression of intimacy. If a Jew called you and used your name twice in this fashion, this person was saying "I have an intimate relationship with you." It is a love relationship signal in the Bible.

Looking at the Old Testament, we see this repetition occur in many places. The story of Abraham and Isaac is found in Genesis 22:1-12 where God says:

> "Take your son, your only child, Isaac, whom you love, and go to the land of Moriah, and offer him there as a burnt offering on one of the mountains where I will tell you." And Abraham rose up early in the morning and saddled his donkey. And he took two of his servants with him, and Isaac his son. And he chopped wood for a burnt offering. And he got up and went to the place which God had told him.
>
> On the third day, Abraham lifted up his eyes, and he saw the place at a distance. And Abraham said to his servants, "You stay here with the donkey, and I and the boy will go up there. We will worship, then we will return to you."
>
> And Abraham took the wood of the burnt offering and placed it on Isaac his son. And he took the fire in his hand and the knife, and the two of them went together. And Isaac said to Abraham his father, "My father!" And he said, "Here I am, my son." And he said, "Here is the fire and the wood, but where is the lamb for a burnt offering?" And Abraham said, 'God will provide the lamb for a burnt offering, my son.' And the two of them went together."

Abraham dutifully follows God's command and prepares to execute Isaac as a sacrifice because God commanded him to do so. I cannot imagine what would be going through Abraham's mind at this time – my long-awaited son, God is asking me to kill him?

Abraham loves God so much that he would sacrifice his only son, but then God intervenes:

> "And they came to the place that God had told him. And Abraham built an altar there and arranged the wood. Then he bound Isaac his son and placed him on the altar atop the wood. And Abraham stretched out his hand and took the knife to slaughter his son. And the angel of Yahweh called to him from heaven and said, 'Abraham, Abraham!' And he said, 'Here I am.'"

Abraham raises the knife, but God calls out to him, "Abraham, Abraham" for him to stop the sacrifice. God was testing Abraham's commitment to Him. God then shows His love for Abraham because He knows that Abraham loves Him in return. He goes on to tell Abraham,

> "Do not stretch out your hand against the boy; do not do anything to him. For now, I know that you are one who fears [loves] God, since you have not withheld your son, your only child, from me" (Genesis 22:11-12).

We see this repeated name pattern occur again in Genesis 46:1-2 when God comes to Jacob in a dream to comfort him about going to Egypt. We see it in Exodus 3:4 when God calls to Moses from the burning bush. We see it in 1 Samuel 3:10 when God calls to Samuel in the night. We see it, painfully, from King David when his son Absalom is killed:

> "The king was deeply moved and went up to the chamber over the gate and wept. And thus, he said as he walked, "O

my son Absalom, my son, my son Absalom! Would I had died instead of you, O Absalom, my son, my son!" (2 Samuel 18:33)

David is so grief stricken that he twice repeats his son's name as well as his position as his son.

In the New Testament, we see the repetition in Luke 10:38-42 in the story of Martha and Mary:

> "Now as they were traveling along, He entered a village; and a woman named Martha welcomed Him into her home. She had a sister called Mary, who was seated at the Lord's feet, listening to His word. But Martha was distracted with all her preparations; and she came up to Him and said, "Lord, do You not care that my sister has left me to do all the serving alone? Then tell her to help me."

> "But the Lord answered and said to her, "**Martha, Martha,** you are worried and bothered about so many things; but only one thing is necessary, for Mary has chosen the good part, which shall not be taken away from her."

Jesus is expressing His love for Martha, knowing her heart of service, and their long, loving relationship.

In Luke 22:31, the Lord says "Simon, Simon, behold, Satan has demanded permission to sift you like wheat."

In Matthew 23:37, Jesus uses the repetition with Jerusalem:

> *"Jerusalem, Jerusalem,* who kills the prophets and stones those who are sent to her! How often I wanted to gather your children together, the way a hen gathers her chicks under her wings, and you were unwilling."

Is there any doubt that the Lord loved Jerusalem and wanted desperately to see her come to Him in faith?

Most powerfully, we see it in Matthew 27:46 where Jesus calls out from the cross:

> About the ninth hour Jesus cried out with a loud voice, saying, "**Eli, Eli,** lama sabachthani?" that is, "**My God, My God**, why have You forsaken Me?"

Jesus, the Son of God, in full knowledge of the Oneness that that He had with the Father, is on the cross saying, "My God, My God" and experiencing a momentary separation of that intimate relationship. I can imagine His unspoken thoughts at this moment: "God, we have this love relationship! Why? WHY? **WHY**, have you forsaken Me?" It is a deep expression of that love.

In Matthew 7:21-23, Jesus said not everyone <u>claiming</u> to have that love relationship with Him will enter Heaven, "but only the one who does the will of My Father who is in heaven."

This is a prophetic statement. It will happen in the future as the Lord is prophesying what is going to happen in the end times. How many people does He say will come to Him? He says, "Many will come to me!" Many will come and say, "Lord! I have an intimate relationship with You." Many of these may be your friends who say they are Christians. However, you observe their lives, and you know they are far away from Christ.

Many will say, "Lord, didn't I come to church? Didn't I do good deeds in Your name? Did I not contribute to a missionary?" Didn't I perform many tasks at church for you? And in your name?" Someone may believe they were a good person in life and are deserving of a place in the Kingdom.

And will He answer back to them?

> "Then I will declare to them, 'I never what knew you.'
> Depart from Me, you who practice lawlessness!"
> (Matthew 7:23).

"I never knew you!" Can you imagine a more chilling statement to hear? "Who are you?" Jesus asks. This answer is the equivalent of knocking at the door to Heaven and having the door slammed in your face or as the modern generation would say "Mic Drop": "I never knew you."

I want to mention, in all seriousness, that if you do not know the Lord, it is truly impossible to love Him. It is impossible to love Him without Him knowing you intimately.

If I meet a lady from the other side of the country in the airport, and this lady is someone whom I have never met, and I immediately run to her and say, "I love you, you know" and she has no idea who I am, she is probably going to run away from me at top speed. "Who IS this guy?" she will say, as she takes off down the concourse.

If you do not know Him, you cannot love him. How important is it to actually know Him?

The Lord mentioned this idea earlier in His ministry, too. In Luke 6:46, He teaches a similar concept to the group in the Sermon on the Mount. "Why do you call me Lord, Lord?" "Why do you say 'Lord, Lord' and do not do what I say?" In other words, how can you say you have a close, intimate, love relationship with Me if you do not obey the commandments? Because "If you love Me, you will obey My commandments" (John 14:15).

In Matthew 15:7-9 Jesus interacts with the Pharisees and said:

> You hypocrites, rightly did Isaiah prophesy of you: 'This people honors Me with their lips, But their heart is far

away from Me.' But in vain do they worship Me, teaching as doctrines the precepts of men (Jesus was quoting Isaiah 29:13ff).

"These people worship me in vanity," Jesus said. "With their lips they sing to me," but their heart is far from Him. Can you imagine such vain worship going on in our generation? Someone is going to church just to check a box. He is singing all the songs, so he must love Jesus! She is taking notes about the sermon, so she must love Him! But he or she has no true, loving relationship with the Lord. If an honest grade were rated on the 0 to 5 scale, the number would be low. That is a challenge to us, my brothers and sisters. We need to look at ourselves and thoroughly consider how we rate on this scale of love for the Lord.

Revelation 2:1-7 records a message to the church at Ephesus, the church where Paul ministered, where Timothy ministered, and where the Apostle John ministered. It was a church of great fruit as Paul noted in the epistle to the Ephesians circa A.D 60-65. As the risen Savior, Jesus has a message for Ephesus in Revelation: "This I have this against you. You have left your first love!" They had left Him! The book of Revelation was written circa A.D. 95-100. The first three chapters in Revelation are not regarded as prophecy to us; they are history to us, as they reflect the Church Age in which we currently live. Therefore, the words to the churches in Revelation 2 and 3 may apply to our churches today.

So, when Jesus sent a message to the Ephesian church, He is also speaking to us. Is He telling us that we have also left our first love? What does He tell the church in Ephesus to do if that is the case? Jesus says, "Repent and do the works you did at first!" In other words, Jesus would say "Go back to the way you lived when you first came to Christ. Go back and study the Bible as you did back then. Go back and commit your life in service like you did then."

He might say, "Remember from whence you came. Remember that loving, heart-committing relationship that flourished in the past. Recommit yourself to Me! Set your heart, like Ezra did, and return to that committed life again...before it's too late."

We should redouble our efforts to love Him, study His Word, support His Church, join His mission, and feed His sheep. Because one day some in our local church might be saying, "Lord, Lord..."

What does Jesus say will happen if Ephesus does not change? "I will come to you and remove your lampstand from its place. Unless you repent." My bride and I have visited the original city of Ephesus. It is no longer a city, it is a ruin. What happened to Ephesus? Their lampstand is gone. The lampstand was ripped out. The church is no more.

If you look at your local church, what do you see? I do not know about you, but I do not want the lampstand of our church to go out. We need to redouble our efforts. We need to shepherd better. We need to teach better. We need to call people to accountability for Christ better. We need to redouble our efforts to do what we did at first. We need to let that fire of love for Jesus shine brightly to all the people around us. It should not only be "head knowledge" but experiential knowledge. We need to live it out day by day.

Christians need to commit to obey Jesus's commandments. In a world where the values of the culture are degrading so quickly, we need to set the example. The Bible is filled with Jesus's words of life. We need to commit to be the examples the world desperately needs.

Christians need to commit to study His Word. Our church places Bible reading guides in the back of our sanctuary every year in January. These guides help a person to read through the Bible each year, not necessarily the detailed study that Ezra was talking about, but just reading the Word. One of our pastors said recently, as he was asked about his personal study time, "You know what I missed? The opportunity to just simply read through the Word – just to read through it for joy of reading it." The psalmist wrote in Psalm 119:111 that reading through the law brings joy. We need to do that.

Christians need to commit to support His Church, both with our time and financial resources. As charitable giving declines across the spectrum of ministries, and the commitment of personal time wanes, we need to set an example of continued support of our churches. Giving should be a product of our love for Him and for others. Only through our dedication will our love be shown to His people and the world.

Christians need to commit to join His Mission in making disciples. We should not only seek to gain knowledge for our own benefit but to be able to share that knowledge with others. We need to dedicate the time to invest in those around us, to build them up, to strengthen their resolve to stand firm in their commitment to Jesus and to be the future examples for the world.

Christians need to commit to feeding His Sheep. As local pastors of our churches or homes, we need to provide spiritual nourishment to our families, provide care and support, and guide our flocks into spiritual maturity.

Commitment

Let today be the day where you recommit your love for God and commit yourself to obey His commandments, to study His word, to support His Church, to share His mission, and to feed His sheep. When you follow this commitment with all your heart, you can be assured that you love the Lord.

If you find yourself lacking in your love for God, let this day be a day of renewal and restoration. God sent His Son to die on the cross for you and for me, for your sins and for mine. Acknowledge that fact and ask Him to forgive you of your sins and bring you into a relationship with Him.

Let this be the prayer of your heart today:

> God, I thank you so much of all the blessings, the manifest blessings that You've given us, Lord. You didn't have to reach down for us. You didn't have to reach down for me.
>
> You didn't have to reach down for us, but You loved us before we were even known, before we were born, and You called us by name. You brought us to a point where we can know the truth in our lives, and You've empowered us to be able to live a certain way through the gift of your Holy Spirit.

Help us, Lord. Help me! Help me to obey and keep your Commandments. Help me, Lord, with the desire and the motivation to study Your Word. Help me, Lord, to give from the heart, not with some mental percentage calculation but out of my deep love for You. Help me to give of my time and my resources to you. Help me to stay on mission, make disciples, and feed Your sheep.

We know all the benefits of these, Lord. They bring us closer to you. They bring us more passionately in love with You, and they bring other people who see us to question why we are so different than others. Oh, that they may ask me, "What's different about you?" and I can share Your light with them. Because I have Your light to give to them.

Help me be committed to that today. Help me to give and serve and study and keep your commandments for the treasure that they are. In the name of Jesus, I pray. Amen.

Appendix A

Introduction to the Bible: A Conversational Tract
(Answering the question, "What's this Bible thing all about?")

I often receive this interesting question, "What's this Bible thing all about?" I usually try to determine whether the individual asking wants a serious answer or just a short and sweet summary.

Sometimes, the short and sweet answer is best: "The Bible is all about a Holy God, in the person of Jesus Christ, coming to earth and dying on the cross as a sacrifice for our sins that we might accept His free gift of grace, so that we are made right with God and rest in this peace, and that we are sanctified on earth, day by day, and that we will be glorified in the future and can live eternally with Him."

However, to some, that answer might not be so short...or sweet. 1 Corinthians 2:12-14 is in the Bible for a reason: a person has to actually have the Spirit's influence on him in order to even begin to grasp or truly understand these ideas.

If the individual truly wants to understand God's plan for the world a little deeper, however, Revelation 12-13 has a longer explanation. From these two chapters, one can receive a summary of the critical message of the Bible.

A hypothetical conversation, with a man named **Bill**, may go something like this:

> Hey Bill, you want to know what the Bible is all about? Well, I have prepared an overview of it for you. If you have deeper questions about some particular items I am going to tell you

about, I can take you to different places in the Bible, but most everything you need to know about the Bible and God's plan is contained in Revelation 12 and 13. These two chapters have God's plan for the world outlined for you. Some of these events have happened in the past, but others are still yet to come. So, Bill, you can know what is in our future!

So, turn in the Bible to Revelation and you can see that these words are not just my words, Bill, but God's words. A man named John was tapped by God to record these words so that anyone may know past and future events for the world because God <u>WANTS</u> us to know what is coming. In the first chapter of this book of Revelation, He says that John should record these words for a purpose and that those who read these words will be blessed.

So, Bill, you have probably heard the story about Adam and Eve of the Bible. God created mankind on the earth so that He could have fellowship with us. The God of the Bible is a relational God; He <u>WANTS</u> you to know Him. That is the high-level goal of our conversation today, Bill. I know Him personally, and I want you to know Him, too.

Turning to Revelation chapter 12, we see God's plan for the world which begins with this sign in Heaven:

"A great sign appeared in heaven: a woman clothed with the sun, and the moon under her feet, and on her head a crown of twelve stars; and she was with child; and she cried out, being in labor and in pain to give birth."

This woman is a symbol of the nation of Israel. Israel was chosen by God for a particular purpose. Israel received special favor in God's eyes; they were simply chosen by God. The Bible said that

Israel was clothed with the sun, had the moon under her feet, and on her head was a crown of 12 stars.

Israel was clothed with the sun, meaning that the nation would show the glory of God to the world. Israel was blessed by God, an honor that God promised to a man named Abraham earlier in the Bible (Genesis 12). The sun and moon together form the entire day; the sun rules the day and the moon rules the night. The crown on Israel's head shows that Israel would have 12 tribes. This picture is also shown in Genesis 37 where a man named Joseph had a dream about it.

The next line says she was "with child." Here is where the story gets interesting. That child was Jesus Christ, the Son of God. God's purpose in choosing Israel was to prepare the world for God to come to earth in the person of Jesus Christ. In the vision the woman is crying out in labor and in pain, about to give birth. When Jesus came into the world over two thousand years ago, Israel was under occupation by Rome. In fact, if you go back thousands of years, Israel has had many moments of being controlled by other worldly powers, and the Jewish people have not always been treated well by the nations of the earth, even in our lifetime. This is all part of God's plan. When Jesus was born, not many people were welcoming. In fact, many people tried to kill Him.

You see, Bill, there is a specific opponent of God who is using every method he can to try to disrupt God's plan. That person is shown in the next few lines in Revelation 12:

"Then another sign appeared in heaven: and behold, a great red dragon having seven heads and ten horns, and on his heads were seven diadems. And his tail swept away a third of the stars

of heaven and threw them to the earth. And the dragon stood before the woman who was about to give birth, so that when she gave birth, he might devour her child."

Another sign in John's vision was a picture of a red dragon. This dragon is Satan, God's main opponent. Throughout the history of the world, Satan has tried to destroy God's plan. He appeared in the Garden of Eden as the serpent trying to distract Adam and Eve from listening to God. He has shown up in other various places in history. Satan is not a real dragon nor is he a human being. He is an angel but he can enter a human being and direct that person to do evil. The Bible actually records that Satan inhabited certain leaders of nations and even one of Jesus' own men named Judas (Isaiah 14; Ezekiel 28, John 13). He could be living inside of a leader in our time, too, although we don't know for sure.

Bill, only a quarter of the people on the earth even believe Satan is a real being. That denial is also part of Satan's plan. He doesn't want people to know he's real. He wants you to believe he is just a fictional character, so you don't know what he is doing. The Bible says that he has a purpose, though: to create havoc on the earth and attack God's people to thwart God's plan (1 Peter 5:8).

The dragon in the Revelation passage has seven heads and ten horns with seven diadems or jeweled crowns on his head. The dragon is a depiction of the world governments Satan has controlled throughout history. In history, the territory where the nation Israel exists has been controlled by 6 specific nations: Egypt, Assyria, Babylon, Media/Persia, Greece, and Rome. The Bible records the story of these nations in many places, but a Biblical prophet named Daniel was given visions about the future of these nations before they were even founded (Daniel 2 and 7).

The Bible has many of these predictions, Bill! One additional world power, though, is yet to come that will rule the nation Israel and other current nations. This will be the 7th head over Israel and the U.S. as well. This world power will split the world into 10 geographic areas which are the 10 horns of the picture. Seven nations wearing seven crowns is the picture of how Satan rules the earth as "the prince of this world" (John 14:30).

The vision shows that the dragon's tail swept away a third of the stars of heaven and threw them to the earth. I mentioned earlier that Satan was an angel. The Bible describes him as the most beautiful angel, and Satan agreed. He wanted to replace God as ruler of Heaven, so he created a rebellion in Heaven. God expelled Satan along with a third of the other angels who were on Satan's side of the mutiny. Satan still had access to come back and forth to Heaven, but he no longer had a home there.

Satan was angry at being kicked out and decided to thwart God's plan to come to earth. Satan, as the dragon, stood by Israel waiting for Jesus Christ to be born so that he could kill Jesus right away. It is something I call the Real War because it affects every other event on earth throughout our past and into our future.

The next line in Revelation 12 describes Jesus' life on earth:

"And she gave birth to a son, a male child, who is to rule all the nations with a rod of iron; and her child was caught up to God and to His throne."

Jesus was born in 3 B.C. and will one day rule all the nations with a rod of iron. A man named King David wrote about this plan before Jesus was born (Psalm 2). In many places in the Bible God's people predicted the story of Jesus's life long before He came to earth. God wanted His people to <u>KNOW</u> that He was coming to visit long before He showed up on the scene. Again, Bill, God wants us to <u>KNOW</u> Him and what His plan is for the earth.

Jesus lived on the earth for about 33 years. You can read about His life in what the Bible calls the gospels: the books of Matthew, Mark, Luke and John. Each one of these books gives a different perspective on Jesus' life on earth. Where all of them share the same perspective, however, is how Jesus was killed by the people of Israel. Some people living at the time in Israel did not understand that Jesus was God coming to visit and believed Jesus to be a fraud. Other people in Israel thought that Jesus was going to take over the world right then, and they didn't like it when He was not what they expected. So, both groups of people came together and determined to kill Jesus.

Of course, the real one behind these actions was Satan because he was determined to thwart God's plan. Satan thought that if Jesus were killed, then God's plan would be over and done. But that is not the way it turned out, Bill. You see, Jesus was God, and He could not be killed. Don't get me wrong, Bill. He did die on a cross. The Romans brutally crucified Him. But He wasn't dead for long. God raised Jesus from the dead three days after He died on a cross. You have probably heard that fact many times. Then He came back to life and appeared in Israel to many people over the next few days. Over 500 people were there when God took Him up to Heaven, right to God's throne (Acts 1). The Bible describes that picture as well, if you are interested (Revelation 4-5). So, right now, Bill, Jesus is seated next to God in Heaven.

Our story in the next line shifts to the future here on earth:

"Then the woman fled into the wilderness where she had a place prepared by God, so that there she would be nourished for one thousand two hundred and sixty days."

This is a future event for Israel. There will be a peace treaty for Israel where the country is protected from their enemies for a time. You probably know that Israel, as a nation, has never really been at peace. They have always lived under occupation or fear of attack from other nations because Satan wants to eliminate Israel from the earth to thwart God's plan. Historically, Satan has tried many times to eliminate Israel. You probably can think of a few events yourself when Jewish people have been kicked out of countries, left abandoned and unprotected. At some moments in Israel's history there was no way the nation should have survived. Right now, they are in conflict with Palestine, Jordan, Iraq, Iran, Saudi Arabia, Russia, and on and on. Even most of the United Nations is against them!

But, in the future, a peace treaty will be signed, and everything will seem like peace has come to Israel. That guy Daniel I was mentioning earlier wrote about this event (Daniel 9) and said there would be an eventual peace agreement. Right now, no temple for God exists in Israel, only something called the Western Wall or the Wailing Wall. A temple will eventually be rebuilt, though, as a gift to Israel as part of that future peace treaty. But the agreement is a fraud, Bill. Israel will be duped into thinking that it is a good deal, but it is not.

Within three and one-half (3 ½) years, Satan will break the agreement and place his own leader in charge of Israel and the temple. Satan will force all the people of the earth to be under this guy's rule, and then, most importantly for Israel, Satan will again attack Israel from within its own borders. When that happens, the Jews will run out of Israel quickly into the hills surrounding the nation. Jesus described this event, too (Matthew 24). God, though, has prepared a place for Israel, and He will take care of them in that mountain area for 3 ½ years or 1,260 days, like the Bible says. At this time on the earth, no one will be able to buy anything unless they have a certain mark on their bodies. Israel will not be able to get any food or supplies at this time, so God will bring His own nourishment for the nation just as He did when He brought the Jewish nation out of Egypt and miraculously provided them with something called manna in the wilderness (Exodus 16).

At this time, 3 ½ years into this fraudulent agreement, Bill, another war will occur as Revelation 12 notes:

"And there was war in heaven, Michael and his angels waging war with the dragon. The dragon and his angels waged war, and they were not strong enough, and there was no longer a place found for them in heaven. And the great dragon was thrown down, the serpent of old who is called the devil and Satan, who deceives the whole world; he was thrown down to the earth, and his angels were thrown down with him."

In this final war in Heaven, Satan and his angels, or demons as we would call them, will be permanently kicked out of Heaven. A very powerful angel named Michael, who is God's general in charge of carrying out His plan, and the good angels will be attacked by Satan and his demons as they try to take over Heaven.

Think about it, Bill. At this time, Satan controls the earth from the temple in Israel, but he wants to control Heaven, too. He and his band of bad guys storm Heaven's gates looking for control.

But Satan will not be strong enough. They will have no place in Heaven, and the whole band will be kicked out and sent back down to the earth.

Satan is described in the Bible in 4 ways. He is called the serpent, a reference to the Garden of Eden with Adam and Eve. He is also called both the devil and Satan. The last name is especially important since he is called "the deceiver of the entire world." Bill, Satan's purpose is to keep you from knowing and having a relationship with God.

- He deceives the world by telling people that God does not exist.

- He deceives the world by teaching people that there are many ways to have a relationship with God, all sorts of "paths" or religions which confuse people and keep them from the truth, like Hinduism and Mormonism, or Taoism or Buddhism.

- He also deceives the world by saying that a person doesn't even have to believe in God; if you are simply a good person and live a good life helping other people, you will be in Heaven. He says that if you do enough good, you will be in Heaven.

- Worst of all, He deceives the world by saying everyone goes to Heaven, regardless of one's beliefs or actions.

But Jesus said that He was the only way to God (John 14:3). It is only through believing in and trusting in Jesus that you can ever truly have a relationship with God. All other ways are frauds and deceptions to keep you from the truth.

The agreement with Israel in the future will also be a fraud and deception. It is meant to deceive Israel so Satan can exterminate the Jews from the Earth.

When Satan and his demons were kicked out of Heaven, a party broke out up there. The next few lines in Revelation 12 tell the story about that party:

Then I heard a loud voice in heaven, saying,

"Now the salvation, and the power, and the kingdom of our God and the authority of His Christ have come, for the accuser of our brethren has been thrown down, he who accuses them before our God day and night."

"And they overcame him because of the blood of the Lamb and because of the word of their testimony, and they did not love their life even when faced with death."

"For this reason, rejoice, O heavens and you who dwell in them. Woe to the earth and the sea, because the devil has come down to you, having great wrath, knowing that he has only a short time."

A loud voice in Heaven announces the party because Satan and his band of demons were defeated and kicked out of Heaven. The people in Heaven who rejoice over this announcement used to live on the earth, Bill. Because they believed in Jesus and trusted Him with their lives, they now live in Heaven with Jesus. Jesus assured these people that they would go to Heaven (John 14).

Satan was accusing them day and night, the Bible says. The Bible records that these accusations are also happening now (Job 1-2; Zechariah 3). But, in the future, God will not hear any accusations against His people. His people overcame the deceptions of Satan, the deceiver of the people, simply because they <u>believed in Jesus</u> and <u>gave personal testimony to the world</u> that they believed Jesus.

The book of Romans discusses how one can be saved (Romans 10:13), Bill, if you call upon the name of the Lord, you can be rescued by Jesus. These people in Heaven may have been killed for believing in Jesus, an event which happened throughout history and still happens today. The story says that these people willingly traded their lives on earth for a life with Jesus in Heaven, even if they faced death. Can you imagine people trusting in their beliefs so much that they were willing to die for them? I do, Bill. I don't fear death here on earth because I know there is a future in Heaven for me.

Let's go back to the Revelation story, Bill. At this time on earth, Satan has been thrown down, and he is not happy about it. While the party is going on in Heaven, the pain is continuing on the earth. The story says that those on the earth will be saying, "Woe", because the devil has been tossed down, and he's mad. Satan only has a certain amount of time before he is ultimately defeated by God. So, Satan will plan to take as many people with him as he can before God shuts him down. Our story continues in the next few lines in Revelation 12:

"And when the dragon saw that he was thrown down to the earth, he persecuted the woman who gave birth to the male child. But the two wings of the great eagle were given to the woman, so that she could fly into the wilderness to her place, where she was nourished for a time and times and half a time, from the presence of the serpent."

When Satan is released back to earth, he starts going after Israel with intense anger. If he can't get God, and he can't get God's people who have already gone to Heaven to be with Him, then he'll try to go after anyone who is still on the earth. The Bible speaks a lot about what life on earth is like at this time (Revelation 6-11). I wouldn't want to be a part of it for sure.

Satan will persecute Israel because Jesus was born from that nation. But, like I mentioned earlier, God will take care of Israel and carry them away to a mountain of safety by a "great eagle." You can imagine that God might use a set of large planes to miraculously transport them to their protected location. Whatever method He chooses, He will take care of them for another 3 ½ years, feed them, and protect them from Satan.

The next few lines in Revelation 12 describe events on earth that will happen to protect Israel:

"And the serpent poured water like a river out of his mouth after the woman, so that he might cause her to be swept away with the flood. But the earth helped the woman, and the earth opened its mouth and drank up the river which the dragon poured out of his mouth."

Satan will use some type of water as a weapon, like perhaps releasing water from a retaining dam to kill Jews from the fleeing Israel. But, the story says, God will cause the earth to remove the water, maybe by an earthquake opening a hole in the earth to take all that water away. You see, Bill, when God has determined to protect His people, nothing will stop Him from doing it. Even the most fiendish plans from Satan cannot stop God from protecting His people. Another book in the Bible called Romans describes God's protection to give His people comfort (Romans 8:28-32).

Now, as you can imagine, Satan is even more enraged that he cannot kill Israel, and the story continues:

"So, the dragon was enraged with the woman, and went off to make war with the rest of her children, who keep the commandments of God and hold to the testimony of Jesus."

Satan cannot get to those who God has protected, so he goes off to find and fight the people that God has not yet carried away. The Bible describes them as the 144,000 witnesses who are "sealed" by God, so they are providentially protected from Satan and his demons (Revelation 7 and 14).

But, Bill, let me stop there. There is a lot more to tell, but you may have heard enough. I want to be conscious of your time, and I know I have taken a good bit of it already.

Are you interested about hearing more of this story? The Bible describes the future for the earth and the people who live on it. Just to give you a preview, though, it's not a pretty scene on earth when Satan is tossed out of Heaven for good. He destroys and attacks anyone he can. God unleashes all sorts of cataclysmic events on the earth to destroy Satan's earthly kingdom and the rest of the world along with it, like earthquakes, diseases, war, and other events that make life on earth horrible for those who are there. But once you die on earth, Bill, you will still come face to face with God (Hebrews 9:27). He will judge only one aspect of every person: is this person God's or does he belong to Satan? Jesus said, "You are either with me or against me" (Matthew 12:30).

Bill, if these events happen in your lifetime, you might be one of those people left on earth and forced to live under these circumstances. I already mentioned to you that I will not be forced to live here if these events happen soon. God will only protect those who are His own people. When you die on earth, you will see God, and the only question will be if you're on His team or not!

You could be His, Bill...! Would you like me to explain to you how you can be one of His people?

Bill, since you want to know more, the story continues in Revelation 13, and gets even more interesting as a new world government is described.

The story reads:

"And the dragon stood on the sand of the seashore. Then I saw a beast coming up out of the sea, having ten horns and seven heads, and on his horns were ten diadems, and on his heads were blasphemous names. And the beast which I saw was like a leopard, and his feet were like those of a bear, and his mouth like the mouth of a lion. And the dragon gave him his power and his throne and great authority.

I saw one of his heads as if it had been slain, and his fatal wound was healed. And the whole earth was amazed and followed after the beast; they worshiped the dragon because he gave his authority to the beast; and they worshiped the beast,

saying, 'Who is like the beast, and who is able to wage war with him?'

There was given to him a mouth speaking arrogant words and blasphemies, and authority to act for forty-two months was given to him. And he opened his mouth in blasphemies against God, to blaspheme His name and His tabernacle, that is, those who dwell in heaven."

Since he has been thrown out of Heaven, Satan is standing on the sand next to a seashore. He has been given almost total control of the earth. Only those who have been sealed by God are able to withstand Satan's assault. Most of the people on the earth have fallen under Satan's deception. The others will be forced to comply or be killed. The beast coming from the sea has a similarity to the dragon from earlier in Revelation. Both have seven heads and ten horns, but there is a difference in that the beast from the sea has ten diadems or jeweled crowns, not 7 like before. In the final world government there will be 10 geographic kingdoms and ten rulers, each with ruling power over his territory. These 10 rulers will be under the control of Satan at the end of the world. Each ruler will have a given name that claims he is God. We do not know what these names will be, but these names will market to the world that they are God and that people should not seek the true God in Heaven.

The beast will have the qualities of a leopard, a bear, and a lion. These animal-like characteristics were described earlier in the Bible to be representative of Babylon, Greece, and Rome (Daniel 7), but this governmental structure will surpass every other one. It will have all the qualities of every past government combined in one menacing force. Think about the worst national government today, Bill. This one will be the worst. It will have the craftiness and agility of a leopard, the crushing power of a bear, and the boasting roar of a lion. Satan will empower this government and give it authority over the world.

Then, Bill, something even more interesting happens in the story. One of the rulers will appear to be killed and then he will be "raised" back to life. This is what happened to Jesus in real life, as we discussed earlier.

Satan is crafty, and he will try to mimic what happened to Jesus with one of these rulers so anyone who might have been reading the Bible during this time will think that this ruler is the returning Jesus. Instead, he is the "Antichrist" – the fake – the copy – the fraud.

What happens because of this event, though, is that the entire world is amazed. "You can live forever," Satan says. It is being covered on CNN and Fox News 24 / 7. The people will fall for the latest deception of Satan and will worship him and the government because he will be seen as the savior of the world. The government will control all the money and all of the religions of the world. Satan will own everything. And the people will say, "I'm on Satan's team because he has all the power"...and he who has the power, makes all the rules.

The beast from the sea, just like Satan, is only given 3 ½ years to reign. Just 42 months and then he and Satan will meet their doom. God will defeat them! During those last 42 months, though, Satan will have his day cursing the true God in Heaven, setting himself up in the temple to be worshipped, and enjoying his reign on earth. Bill, you remember when I mentioned that Satan was thrown out of Heaven initially because he wanted to be God? His pride and arrogance wanted all the praise. Well,

Bill, Satan finally gets his wish - on earth – just like he wanted. But it will only last for 42 months.

The story continues in Revelation 13:

"It was also given to him to make war with the saints and to overcome them, and authority over every tribe and people and tongue and nation was given to him. All who dwell on the earth will worship him, everyone whose name has not been written from the foundation of the world in the book of life of the Lamb who has been slain. If anyone has an ear, let him hear. If anyone is destined for captivity, to captivity he goes; if anyone kills with the sword, with the sword he must be killed. Here is the perseverance and the faith of the saints."

Satan will be allowed by God to overpower some of His people. God will allow them to be killed, and He will bring them to Heaven. Satan will be given authority over everyone on the earth, every tribe and people and every tongue and nation. Satan will control Israel, culture, all nations and racial groups. He will own it all. Everyone will worship him except for those who believe in Jesus and are on God's team. This is what the Bible means when it says, "written from the foundation of the world in the book of life of the Lamb who has been slain."

That lamb was Jesus, Bill. Only those who have a relationship with Jesus will survive. The Lamb is seen earlier in the Bible (Revelation 4 and 5) as being in Heaven because God took Him up to be next to His throne. If you are one of God's people, you will avoid this rule of Satan on earth. God knows who His people are, Bill, but sometimes His people don't know they are on God's team. This is why I'm sharing this story with you, Bill. You could be one of God's people, but you just do not know it yet!

But we are not done with the Revelation 13 story because there is another beast coming:

"Then I saw another beast coming up out of the earth; and he had two horns like a lamb and he spoke as a dragon. He exercises all the authority of the first beast in his presence. And he makes the earth and those who dwell in it to worship the first beast, whose fatal wound was healed. He performs great signs, so that he even makes fire come down out of heaven to the earth in the presence of men. And he deceives those who dwell on the earth because of the signs which it was given him to perform in the presence of the beast, telling those who dwell on the earth to make an image to the beast who had the wound of the sword and has come to life."

This beast that shows up next on the earth is a marketing guy. He will be constantly reminding the people of the greatness of the government. The writer of Revelation called him the false prophet. He will only have 2 horns, not the 10 horns of the government, so he will have lesser power. He will be seen as a gentle ruler, but he is still powered by Satan. He will market the government's greatness through persuasion, not by force like the prior beast. Jesus described both of these leadership styles in the Bible (Matthew 20:25).

This marketing guy will be a great magician, too. He will be able to show great magical tricks to convince the world of his authenticity. The people will be amazed at this guy, and he will point everyone to the government and its leaders just like Satan wants. He will convince the people on earth to make images of the ruler who was seemingly killed and restored to life. He will convince people that this ruler is the returning Jesus. He will even convince some of the people of Israel that this is the Jesus from

166

the Bible! Jesus predicted this ruler would come (Matthew 24:24). They will call this guy the long-awaited Messiah, the savior of Israel. You will remember I mentioned that they were expecting this type of ruler when Jesus showed up, but they killed Him because He didn't do what they expected. Well, Bill, this ruler who died and came back to life <u>WILL</u> be the guy that they like, and everyone will fall for his deception. It's a trick.

What is great about Jesus and the Bible, Bill, is that He told His people ahead of time that these events would happen (Matthew 24) so they could be prepared and not be deceived by Satan and his tricksters.

The story goes on a little further in Revelation 13:

"And it was given to him to give breath to the image of the beast, so that the image of the beast would even speak and cause as many as do not worship the image of the beast to be killed.

And he causes all, the small and the great, and the rich and the poor, and the free men and the slaves, to be given a mark on their right hand or on their forehead, and he provides that no one will be able to buy or to sell, except the one who has the mark, either the name of the beast or the number of his name.

Here is wisdom. Let him who has understanding calculate the number of the beast, for the number is that of a man; and his number is six hundred and sixty-six."

This is the end of the story of Satan's rule of the earth. The government will give the people a choice: they can worship the government or be killed by the government. The same event happened earlier in the nation Babylon where King

Nebuchadnezzar made a statue and forced the people to worship the statue or be thrown into the furnace and be burned alive (Daniel 3).

In this latest government the method of execution might be different, or it might be the same. We do not know the method for sure, but we do know that everyone left on earth will face the choice.

To further his argument, Satan and his government will force every person on the earth, no matter how rich or powerful, to have a specific mark in order to be able to buy or sell merchandise. Without this mark, a person will die slowly without food or other supplies. With the mark, a person will live in the modern world but will align himself with Satan and his demons. The mark will have different forms. One will be based on the government's name and the other a specific number aligning to the government's leader. In essence, these marks serve the same purpose: a person will either be a part of the world system or out of it. Most people on the earth will be in it, rationalizing that they need to be in to survive and that this mark is the only way to do it.

This will be the choice you may have to make, Bill, if you're still on the earth. You probably have heard the phrase "sell your soul to the devil" in order to gain something. Well, if you are around at this time on the earth, that is what you will have to do to live. It will be your only option. You will face constant pressure from the marketing guy: "You need to be plugged into the government system or else, die slowly of starvation."

You have also heard of the devil being aligned to the number 666. There have been more theories on the number 666 than the stars in the sky. People have taken this calculation as a challenge. "Ooooh," they say, "you can calculate the guy's name from his number!" They use all sorts of methods of changing letters into numerical replacements and have determined that this person's name was the name of many kings of the past. I'm sure some current national leaders are on the list, too. These people continue to say, "This is the one!"

But let's be clear about this, Bill. The world leader has not shown up on the scene in the world yet, and when he does, everyone will know who he is. This guy will <u>WANT</u> everyone to know who he is. He will be arrogant and prideful and will command attention. But, remember, there are events that must happen before this guy is made known to the world.

Remember, a peace treaty will be made between Israel and the nations around it to rebuild the temple. This peace treaty will be the sign that these events are coming to fruition on the earth. When that peace treaty is signed, then people on the earth should begin to look for the name and number of 666. Until then, any speculation about who he is will be just a waste of time.

The larger question, Bill, is whether you want to be with God in Heaven or on earth during this dangerous time when Satan rules. You can be <u>sure</u> to avoid all these events by being on God's team right now.

If these events happen in your lifetime, you might be one of those people left on earth and forced to live under these circumstances. I already mentioned to you that I will not be forced to live here if these events happen a few years from now. I'm telling you that God will only protect those who are on His team. When you die on earth, you will see God, and the question will be: are you on His team or not?

You could be His, Bill...! Would you like me to explain to you how you can be one of His people?

May many be approached and make a decision to accept Jesus Christ in your use of this conversational tract.

Another Book from VEA Publishing

Pastor Timothy Lusk shares a collection of personal poems and prayers mined from a lifetime of service to the people of God's kingdom. Throughout his career as a pastor and counselor, he has sought comfort in poetry crafted especially for himself and those he has assisted along life's journeys.

As you read through and contemplate his creations, you will find peace in the knowledge that the steps of your personal journey, while always unique to you, are shared among many others who have walked similar paths with the same need for love, comfort, and understanding.

Timothy Lusk is the Senior Pastor of Eastside Community Church in Jacksonville, Florida.

He has served as a Pastor in several churches in the Jacksonville community over a 40+ year ministry career and founded Redemptive Leadership International (RLI), a ministry organization created to equip and empower transformational leaders for Christ's redemptive purposes around the world.

He is a graduate of Dallas Theological Seminary (Masters of Theology). Timothy and his wife Allison have three children: James, Ben, and Mary as well as four grandchildren.

Go to www.veapublishing.com/orders to purchase Timothy's book.

VEA Publishing
P.O. Box 50235
Jacksonville Beach, Florida 32240

www.veapublishing.com

Made in the USA
Coppell, TX
27 June 2021

58202998R00098